S70

ACPL ITEM
DISCARDED

P9-ELH-318

4-17-79

God
With
Us

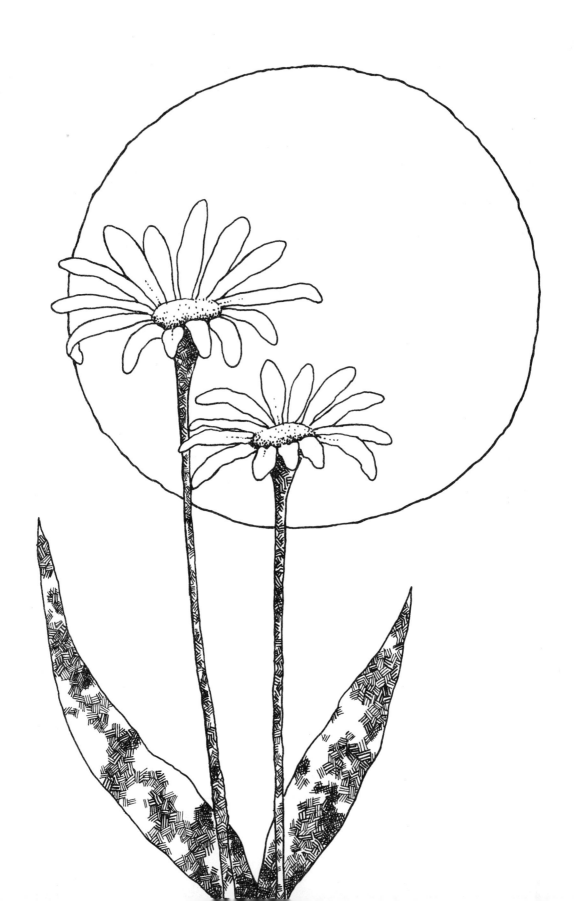

God-With-Us

Resources for Prayer and Praise

MIRIAM THERESE WINTER

Abingdon—Nashville

042

79 8749 4

GOD-WITH-US

Copyright © 1979 by the Medical Mission Sisters, Philadelphia, PA 19111

All rights reserved.
No part of this book may be reproduced in any manner
whatsoever without written permission of the publisher
except brief quotations embodied in critical articles
or reviews. For information address Abingdon,
Nashville, Tennessee

Library of Congress Cataloging in Publication Data

WINTER, MIRIAM THERESE.
God with us.
   1.   Worship programs.   I.   Title.
BV198.W56   264'.02   78-13616

ISBN 0-687-15300-X

Scripture quotations in this publication unless otherwise noted are from
the Revised Standard Version Common Bible, copyrighted © 1973 by the
Division of Christian Education of the National Council of the Churches of
Christ in the U.S.A., and are used by permission.

Scripture quotations noted TEV are from Today's English Version of the
Bible. Copyright © American Bible Society 1966, 1971.

Scripture quotations noted JB are from The Jerusalem Bible, copyright ©
1966 by Darton, Longman & Todd, Ltd. and Doubleday & Company, Inc.
Used by permission of the publisher.

Scripture quotations noted Phillips are from The New Testament in
Modern English, copyright © J. B. Phillips 1958, 1960, 1972.

Scripture quotations marked with an asterisk have been adapted by the
author.

Additional acknowledgments are on page 112.

MANUFACTURED BY THE PARTHENON PRESS AT
NASHVILLE, TENNESSEE, UNITED STATES OF AMERICA

2053992

Contents

At every turn life links us to the Lord!

(Rom. 14:8 Phillips)

Preface

The signs are all around us. At every turn, the Scripture says, life links us to the Lord. The connection is not always apparent. It is sometimes hard to see a sequence of meaning in the meaningless mess we make, hard to make sense of the senseless threats of these terrifying times. Yet the times often catch us listening for one clear, unambiguous Word, for assurance that we will live happily ever after, that there is more than meets the eye. Our certainty: God-with-us, a presence in our midst.

Every attempt to touch transcendence, tentatively or boldly believing, is an acknowledgment of God-with-us and a personal claim on us. Whenever we wait for something, extend an invitation, celebrate a birth or a birthday, we experience a beginning and participate in that genesis of our in-the-beginning God. As we come to terms with turning points, hunger and thirst for justice or the necessities of life, succumb to doubt or desperation or the black night of despair, we reflect that incomprehensible paradox of a helpless, crucified God, endure that empty absurdity essential to the triumph of the tomb. Bittersweet. Breakthrough! With every taste of freedom, every hesitant "forgive me," every time we gift or are gifted or dare to reveal our names, it is Easter. Again. Beginnings, resurrections, the power to deal with paradox, all of this is possible because of bedrock values that stabilize our lives: those promises we make and keep; the sinking of deep, insistent roots; the myriad times we make, mean, love. These pivotal points on which life turns link us to the Lord and prepare us for returning, help us to overcome our fear of finally coming home. We had nothing in the beginning. We must yield all in the end, return all borrowed wonders gratefully to their source. Returning means becoming adept at the delicate art of letting go. Which is in fact a beginning. We are always beginning again.

The following pages flow from the conviction that life is liturgy and that liturgy is life. These services and songs and reflections make celebration moments of significant turning points. Emerging from the mundane yet not bound by its limitations, they mix up the sacred and secular after the manner of our incarnate Lord, to test how well we are integrating our behavior and our belief. Prayer that is reality-oriented is our best resource for praise, complimenting the God who, in the beginning, made everything very good. To encourage creative additions, many of the modules offered here are purposely incomplete. Expand the outlines. Edit them. Mix and match the pieces. See how the bittersweet Lenten mood relates to later darkness, how the breakthrough of Easter and Pentecost permeates the year. This source book is a companion volume to *Preparing the Way of the Lord,* which assists praying communities in shaping their collective prayer.

If you simply skim the surface, you might miss entirely the centrality of the Cross. That prelude to Resurrection is a wound too deep for words. We catch its pale reflection in all the innocent suffering undeserved and unexplained that time and again tests our commitment with the force of its assertion: life is healthy when it hurts. Why are we put to death day after day? To know more and more of life, to prepare for that ultimate dying and the final beginning again.

It is tough to be festive, to celebrate existence while struggling to survive. Yet this is what God asks of us amid the distraction of contemporary clutter, amid the temptation to yield to terror and ridicule belief. God asks that we turn to a presence permanently in our midst. There we will find the courage to cope with anxiety and those things we cannot change, gain strength to handle surprises or boredom or stress. "Turn and be healed" (Isa. 6:10). Prophetic words. Comforting words. At every turn, as we spiral through our seasons, through the pain of winter and the promise of spring, as we deepen, ripen, mature, we draw nearer to that presence we desire with all our heart. "At every turn life links us to the Lord" (Rom. 14:8 Phillips). Prayer is turning to God. Come, then. Let us pray!

Beginnings

Starting points
where something begins
again
and again
mark our rites of passage,
link seasons in time
to seasons of prayer
and the seasons of the heart.
Advent-to-Christmas
defines us
more than we'll ever know.
Longing, looking forward,
first steps
a second chance . . .
we are always pregnant,
shape and are shaped by
courage, hope,
for the facts of faith and flesh.
Time
the timeless eternal:
that which we bring to birth
brings us back
to our beginnings
and helps us
begin
again.

Waiting

Sit together in silence for several minutes. When the group begins to get uneasy because of the unexplained wait, the leader starts to read the selection from Anthony Padovano's Dawn Without Darkness.

Leader	Nothing worthwhile in life is sudden. We wait for birth. We wait for love. We wait for life to reveal its meaning, year by year, experience by experience. Waiting is the law of life, the measure of love. (A. Padovano)
Reading	The Lord gave me this answer: "Write down clearly on tablets what I reveal to you, so that it can be read at a glance. Put it in writing, because it is not yet time for it to come true. But the time is coming quickly, and what I show you will come true. It may seem slow in coming, but wait for it; for it will certainly take place, and it will not be delayed. And this is the message: 'Those who are evil will not survive, but those who are righteous will live because they are faithful to God.' " (Hab. 2:2-4 TEV)
Leader	To wait for another person is to be willing to be alone. . . . To wait for someone is to say that the present does not begin until he [or she] arrives. To wait together with another is to form a community of hope . . . to affirm the need for another person or a further value essential to the togetherness of those who are vigilant. (A. Padovano)
Reading	I consider that what we suffer at this present time cannot be compared at all with the glory that is going to be revealed to us. All of creation waits with eager longing for God to reveal his sons [and daughters]. For creation was condemned to lose its purpose, not of its own will, but because God willed it to be so. Yet there was the hope that creation itself would one day be set free from its slavery to decay and would share the glorious freedom of the children of God. For we know that up to the present time all of creation groans with pain, like the pain of childbirth. But it is not just creation alone which groans; we who have the Spirit as the first of God's gifts also groan within ourselves as we wait for God to make us sons [and daughters] and set our whole being free. For it was by hope that we were saved; but if we see what we hope for, then it is not really hope. For who hopes for something he [or she] sees? But if we hope for what we do not see, we wait for it with patience. (Rom. 8:18-25 TEV)
Leader	Many times we wonder why life has to take so much time, why it must move forward step by step, moment by moment. If we try to rush it, it goes wrong. Life has its own time to keep, its own unhurried pace to set. And so we learn to wait. (A. Padovano)

Reflection on Waiting. All recite together, slowly, the following passage:

Waiting . . . waiting . . . for water to boil . . . for the phone to ring . . . for the end of a day . . . for friends to come . . . for the sun to rise . . . for a rose to open . . . for a hurt to heal . . . for a child to be born . . . for war to end . . . for dawn to break . . . for thunder to crack . . . for a tear to fall . . . for the motor to start . . . for an egg to hatch . . . for wheat to ripen . . . for school to end . . . for a fish to bite . . . for the stock market to rise . . . for the return of a son . . . for a marriage proposal . . . for the tide to recede . . . for death to come . . . for a thought to jell . . . for a tree to topple . . . for a sign of love . . . for a balloon to burst . . . for a letter from home . . . for an earthquake to stop . . . for a bee to sting . . . for the washer to complete its cycle . . . for the first snowfall . . . for a speech to end . . . for the gasp of a drowned child . . . for ink to dry . . . for a decision to be made . . . for a strike to end . . . for the astronauts' splashdown . . . for the game to begin . . . for a better world . . . for a child to crawl . . . for the sobriety of an alcoholic . . . for the bread to rise . . . for a fog to clear . . . for a plane to land . . . for a sign of hope . . . for corn to pop . . . for the ambulance to come . . . for the future to be revealed . . . for a silence to fall . . . "I waited and waited for the Lord. Now at last he has stooped to me" (Ps. 40). (Frank Galles)

Sit Silently in prayer for several minutes.

All   We wait for everything that is really worth having.
                We wait to be born. We wait for love to touch us.
                We wait for life to grow. Till the very end, we wait.
                We even wait for God.   (A. Padovano)

Come!

Come, Lord Jesus + Come, Lord Jesus + Come, Lord

Reading   I, Jesus, have sent my angel to make these revelations to you for the sake of the churches. I am of David's line, the root of David and the bright star of the morning. The Spirit and the Bride say, "Come." Let everyone who listens answer, "Come." Then let all who are thirsty come: all who want it may have the water of life and have it free. The one who guarantees these revelations repeats his promise: I shall indeed be with you soon. Amen; come, Lord Jesus! May the grace of the Lord Jesus be with you all. Amen. (Rev. 22: 16-17, 20-21 JB)

Reading and Response.   This selection is from the writings of the Bengali poet Rabindranath Tagore. Let one person read the verses, and everyone join in on the response.

Have you not heard his silent steps?
> *All:* He comes, comes, ever comes.

Every moment and every age, every day and every night,
> *All:* He comes, comes, ever comes.

Many a song have I sung in many a mood of mind,
but all their notes have always proclaimed,
> *All:* He comes, comes, ever comes.

In the fragrant days of sunny April through the forest path,
> *All:* He comes, comes, ever comes.

In the rainy gloom of July nights
on the thundering chariot of clouds,
> *All:* He comes, comes, ever comes.

In sorrow after sorrow,
it is his steps that press upon my heart,
and it is the golden touch of his feet
that makes my joy to shine.

Commentary   He comes, comes, ever comes. The Lord is always coming, even when he is here. He has come, does come, will come again—today, tomorrow, at the last sunset when he will gather his children home. We are reminded to seek the Lord "while he is still to be found, call to him while he is still near" (Isa. 55:6 JB). We call out without hesitation: Come, Lord Jesus, come!

Song   "Long Is Our Winter" (by the Grail, page 54) or Miriam Therese Winter's "Child of Morning"

Child of Morning

Words and music by
Sister Miriam Therese Winter

1. Sing a song to the Child of Morn-ing, sing for the King is com-ing. To the maid to whom he was born, sing to her brave be-com-ing. Sing of a peace he will bring a-gain, peace and fel-low-ship. Praise him then! Sing glo-ry to God in the high-est.

2. Sing a song to the Child of Sor-row, sing for the dream re-turn-ing. Love to-day and laugh to-mor-row, sing for the things we're learn-ing. Love, the in-vis-i-ble, now ap-pears, with time to be ten-der and time for tears. Sing glo-ry to God in the high-est.

3. Sing a song to the Child of Morn-ing, sing for the child that's cry-ing. Big black head-lines scream a warn-ing... sing for the dead and dy-ing. The Child of the Morn-ing must be slain, yet a sliv-er of light and hope re-main. Sing glo-ry to God in the high-est.

© MCMLXXI by Medical Mission Sisters, Phil., Pa.
Reprinted by permission Vanguard Music Corp., W. 57th St., N.Y., N.Y. 10019

A Litany of Invitation to the Lord Who Comes
    Divide the community into two groups, group A and group B. Pray the litany aloud as a two-part choir, with everyone joining in on the response.

A: Come in a whirlwind! Awaken awareness!
B: Come in a still breeze, speak to our hearts.
                    All: Come, Lord Jesus, come!

A: Come, lift the clouds, enlighten our darkness.
B: Come, gentle Presence, come as a friend.
                    All: Come, Lord Jesus, come!

A: Come, perfect peace, long, long promised.
B: Come, heal our brokenness, bind up our wounds.
                    All: Come, Lord Jesus, come!

A: Come, lead us safely through our wilderness wanderings.
B: Come, shade, come, shelter: stretch out your hand.
                    All: Come, Lord Jesus, come!

A: Come, Bread of Life, the whole world hungers.
B: Come, Living Water! How long must we thirst?
                    All: Come, Lord Jesus, come!

A: Come, Liberator! Lead us from bondage!
B: Come, Justice, restore the lost rights of the poor.
                    All: Come, Lord Jesus, come!

A: Come, banish mourning, set our hearts dancing.
B: Come quickly! You are our strength and our song.
                    All: Come, Lord Jesus, come!

A: Come, Life! Come, Easter! Come, Love, come alive in us.
B: Come, Christ! Come, Christmas! Come, Life, become love in us.
                    All: Come, Lord Jesus, come!

Silent Reflection

Prayer   God our Father,
           the One who has come in your name
           comes again
           with majesty and power,
           with decisiveness and strength,
           with integrity and imagination,
           with gentleness and peace.
           May he enter the hearts of those who wait
           with quiet expectation
           for all that is good and holy and just. Amen

Benediction   May the One who comes
                become in us
                love-made-visible to all.
                Amen.
    The group might like to conclude with song: "Maranatha" by Lucien Deiss or "Come, Lord Jesus" by Miriam Therese Winter.

Advent wreath

Advent is a time of expectation, of preparing the way of the Lord. It has become customary in many homes and communities to gather daily around a wreath of greens and candles to pray, Come, Lord Jesus! The candles measure the waiting during those long, long weeks before Christmas. One lone candle burns the first week, two the second week, three the third, and four during that final week, reminding us not only of the world's long wait for a Messiah, but of our own impatient longing for the One who came, who comes, and who will come again. An Advent wreath is easy to make. Take a deep round tray or pie plate and place four candles in it, three the color of lavender and one of rose. Fill the plate with water, and arrange bits of green around the candles—small pine branches, holly, boxwood hedge or spruce. Place the wreath on the dining room table or wherever the family gathers for its evening meal.

First Week
On Saturday evening, the vigil before the First Sunday of Advent, gather around the wreath just before dinner. Sing one verse of the carol, "O Come, O Come, Emmanuel" as indicated below, or recite the verse together.

Song "O Come, O Come, Emmanuel" (Latin carol, ninth century)

> O Come, O come, Emmanuel, and ransom captive Israel,
> That mourns in lonely exile here until the Son of God appear.
>   Rejoice! Rejoice! O Israel, to you shall come Emmanuel.

After the song, the youngest child lights one candle, and then another family member prays the following prayer.

Prayer Stir up your power, O Lord our God, and come.
> Brighten our hearts with the glad hope
> of your presence in our midst.
> We wait unafraid for that Light in our darkness
> who is Jesus Christ the Lord. Amen.

Plan to repeat this prayer/action every night of the coming week as a blessing before the evening meal. Take turns lighting the candle and leading the prayer each night.

Second Week
On Saturday evening before the Second Sunday of Advent, everyone sings or recites a new verse, as indicated below.
Song "O Come, O Come, Emmanuel" (verse two)

> O Come now, Wisdom from on high, who orders all things mightily;

To us the path of knowledge show, and teach us
    in her ways to go.
Rejoice! Rejoice! O Israel, to you shall come Emmanuel.
After the song, the youngest child lights two candles, adding a new candle to the one that has been burning all week. Then another member leads the prayer.

Prayer   Stir up your power, O Lord our God, and come.
    We eagerly await the Christmas miracle
    of Love-made-flesh like us.
    Help us to love one another more and more
    in Jesus Christ our Lord. Amen.

Repeat this prayer/action every night of the second week of Advent. Take turns lighting the candles and leading the prayer.

Third Week

On Saturday evening before the Third Sunday of Advent, everyone sings or recites a new verse, as indicated below.

Song   "O Come, O Come, Emmanuel" (verse three)

    O come now, Dayspring from on high, and cheer us
        by your drawing nigh;
    Disperse the gloomy clouds of night, and death's dark
        shadow put to flight.
    Rejoice! Rejoice! O Israel, to you shall come Emmanuel.

After the song, the youngest child lights the rose-colored candle to announce Gaudete, the joyful week of Advent. When the candles of the two previous weeks have also been lit, a family member leads the prayer.

Prayer   Stir up your power, O Lord our God, and come.
    We wait together, rejoicing
    in the promise of your birth.
    There is room in our hearts for you.
    We welcome you today and every day.
    Come, Lord Jesus, come! Amen.

Repeat this prayer/action every night of the third week of Advent. Take turns lighting the candles and leading the prayer.

Fourth Week

On Saturday evening before the Fourth Sunday of Advent, everyone sings or recites a new verse, as indicated below.

Song   "O Come, O Come, Emmanuel" (verse four)

    O come, Desire of nations, bind as one, the hearts
        of all mankind;
    Bid all our sad divisions cease, and be yourself
        our King of Peace.
    Rejoice! Rejoice! O Israel, to you shall come Emmanuel.

After the song, the youngest child lights all four candles. Then another member of the family leads the prayer.

Prayer   Stir up your power, O Lord our God, and come.
    Bring peace to our home and family,
    and to families all over the earth.
    We long to know this Prince of Peace
    who is Jesus Christ the Lord. Amen.

Repeat this prayer/action until Christmas Eve, adding the O Antiphons on the appropriate days, as explained below.

O Antiphons

The great O Antiphons, sung by the church before and after the vespers Magnificat during the final octave before Christmas, are among the most beautiful elements in the Advent liturgy. Already in use by the eighth century, they may well reach back into much earlier times, a link to our liturgical past. Let us also gather each evening before Christmas and dare to address the One who will come by these splendid, revealing names: Wisdom, Lord of lords, Root of Jesse, Key of David, Rising Sun, King of nations, God-with-us (Emmanuel).

On December 17 and the remaining days before Christmas, extend the evening Advent wreath blessing to include the O Antiphon of the day, the Magnificat, and a summary prayer. As we call on the Lord each evening, we ask for a share of the blessing that each title proclaims and increase our sense of excitement and anticipation as Christmas draws very near.

First Day (December 17)

Copy out the antiphon in large letters so that it can be seen and recited by all. Hang it on the refrigerator, so that it can be remembered and prayed often throughout the following day. Try making symbols: root, key, sun, and so forth.

O Wisdom, who proceeds from the mouth of the Most High, reaching from beginning to end, mightily and sweetly ordering all things: Come and teach us the way of prudence!

The Magnificat can be read from your favorite Scripture translation or in the metrical version below. If you prefer to sing it, try the setting by Joseph Gelineau, a Grail publication, or this text to the haunting hymn tune on page 19.

My soul gives glory to the Lord.
My heart pours out its praise.
God lifted up my lowliness
in many marvelous ways.

The Lord has done great things for me:
Holy is this Name.
All people will declare me blessed,
and blessings they shall claim.

From age to age, to all who fear,
such mercy Love imparts,
dispensing justice far and near,
dismissing selfish hearts.

The Magnificat

Sister Miriam Therese Winter

Wyeth's *Repository of Sacred Music*

1. My soul gives glo - ry ___ to the ___ Lord. My
2. The Lord has done great ___ things for ___ me:
3. From age to age, to ___ all who ___ fear, such
4. Love casts the might - y ___ from their ___ thrones, pro -
5. The Lord is true to ___ Is - ra - el, a -

heart pours out its praise. God ___
Ho - ly is this Name. All ___
mer - cy Love im - parts, dis -
motes the in - se - cure, leaves ___
lert to ev - 'ry need, re -

lif - ted ___ up my low - li - ness in
peo - ple ___ will de - clare me ___ blessed, and
pens - ing ___ jus - tice far and ___ near, dis -
hun - gry ___ spir - its sat - is - fied, the
mem - ber - ing past prom - is - es to

man - y mar - vel - ous ways.
bless - ings they ___ shall claim.
miss - ing sel - fish hearts.
rich seem sud - den - ly poor.
A - bra - ham and ___ his seed.

Copyright © 1978 by Medical Mission Sisters, Phil., Pa.

Love casts the mighty from their thrones,
promotes the insecure,
leaves hungry spirits satisfied,
the rich seem suddenly poor.

The Lord is true to Israel,
alert to every need,
remembering past promises
to Abraham and his seed.

Repeat: O Wisdom . . .
Leader: Let us pray.
   O the depth of the riches and wisdom
   and knowledge of God!
   You possessed wisdom, O Lord,
   in the beginning of your ways,
   chose what is foolish
   to shame the wise.
   Come and teach us
   the subtle wisdom of the Cross,
   through Jesus Christ our Lord. Amen.

Second Day (December 18)

O Lord of lords and Leader of the house of Israel, who appeared to Moses in the fire of the burning bush and gave him the Law on Sinai: Come and redeem us by your outstretched arm.

Recite or sing the Magnificat.

Repeat: O Lord of Lords . . .

Leader: Let us pray.
   O Lord of lords,
   fire in the burning bush,
   descending upon us in tongues of flame,
   we approach you in awe yet all the while
   we dare to say: Our Father.
   You who gave us Law and Spirit,
   teach us to know where one ends
   and the other carries on.
   Come now among us with gentle burning
   and redeem us with your outstretched arm,
   through Jesus Christ your Son. Amen.

Third Day (December 19)

O Root of Jesse, emblem of the people,
   before whom kings keep silent,
   to whom nations pray:
   come deliver us. Do not delay!

Recite or sing the Magnificat.

Repeat: O Root of Jesse . . .

Leader: Let us pray.
   O Root of Jesse,
   ground of being,

in whom we sink our rootlessness,
lift us beyond our stunted dreams
as we struggle to cherish our sources
and bring forth good fruit in your name. Amen.

Fourth Day   (December 20)

O Key of David and Scepter of the house of Israel,
who opens and no one closes,
who closes and no one dares to open:
Come and free those who are imprisoned
in darkness and in the shadow of death.

Recite or sing the Magnificat.

Repeat: O Key of David . . .

Leader: Let us pray.
O Key of David,
Door of the Kingdom,
Gateway to peace,
free us from the prisons of our locked lives.
Batter our hearts, three-personed God,
until we hear your word
and respond to need
openly, without reserve. Amen.

Fifth Day   (December 21)

O Rising Sun, Splendor of eternal Light and Sun of Justice:
Come and enlighten those who sit in darkness
and in the shadow of death.

Sing or recite the Magnificat.

Repeat: O Rising Sun . . .

Leader: Let us pray.
O Rising Sun,
Dawn of Salvation,
Splendor of eternal Light,
enlighten our darkness now, quickly,
you who are Christ,
Messiah and Lord,
Sun of Justice. Amen.

Sixth Day   (December 22)

O King of nations, the Desired of all,
the Cornerstone that unites:
Come and save the people you created out of clay.

Recite or sing the Magnificat.

Repeat: O King of nations . . .

Leader: Let us pray.
O King of nations,
Cornerstone of all that we desire,

authority over everything we do and are,
make of all nations
one family on earth
and rule gently with compassion and peace.
May your Kingdom come!
Now and always,
we pray in your name. Amen.

Seventh Day   (December 23)
O Emmanuel, our King and Lawgiver, the
Expectation and Savior of the nations:
Come and save us, O Lord our God!

Recite or sing the Magnificat.

Repeat: O Emmanuel . . .

Leader: Let us pray.
O Emmanuel,
God-with-us in the cool of the evening,
guiding with pillars of cloud and fire,
forming a covenant of friendship
as promise of a lasting bond,
continue with us on our journey
through darkness, disappointment, doubt,
for you are the way, the truth, life,
now and forever. Amen.

Christmas Eve   (December 24)
It is Christmas Eve, the moment long awaited. Gather one more time around the wreath to call on the Lord so near at hand. Light all four candles, sing a favorite carol, and join in the following prayer.

Leader: O Wisdom, who proceeds from the mouth of the Most
High, reaching from beginning to end, mightily and
sweetly ordering all things:
All: Come and teach us the way of prudence!

Leader: O Lord of lords and Leader of the house of Israel,
who appeared to Moses in the fire of the burning
bush and gave him the Law on Sinai:
All: Come and redeem us by your outstretched arm.

Leader: O Root of Jesse, emblem of the people, before whom
kings keep silent, to whom nations pray:
All: Come deliver us. Do not delay!

Leader: O Key of David and Scepter of the house of Israel,
who opens and no one closes, who closes
and no one dares to open:
All: Come and free those who are imprisoned
in darkness and in the shadow of death.

Leader: O Rising Sun, Splendor of eternal Light and Sun of Justice:
All: Come and enlighten those who sit in darkness
and in the shadow of death.

Leader: O King of nations, the Desired of all,
the Cornerstone that unites:

All: Come and save the people you created out of clay.

Leader: O Emmanuel, our King and Lawgiver, the Expectation
and Savior of the nations:

All: Come and save us, O Lord our God.

Leader: Let us pray.
O Son of God, our Savior,
today we await your coming,
and tomorrow we shall see your glory.
Reveal the good news to all of us
who long for your arrival.
Come, Love incarnate, do not delay.
Come, Lord Jesus! Amen.

Christmas Tree

The tree is a sign and symbol of life, of fidelity, of salvation. Season by season, it unfolds its potential through deprivation, rebirth, ripeness—reaching out beyond its limitations, embracing every whim of weather, sinking deep, satisfying roots into its ground of being. Each year at Christmas, a tree reminds us of who we are and of what God has done for us. Gather with family and friends around your untrimmed tree. The following ceremony will help you experience the wealth of meaning within this traditional Christmas symbol as you prepare its place of honor in your home.

Song "O Christmas Tree" (traditional German folk song)

O Christmas tree, O Christmas tree,
  A tree most fair and lovely. (Repeat)
Your shining green at Christmastide
Spreads hope and gladness far and wide.
O Christmas tree, O Christmas tree,
  A tree most fair and lovely.

O Christmas tree, O Christmas tree,
  You have a wondrous message: *(Repeat)*
For you proclaim the Savior's birth,
Good will to all and peace on earth.
O Christmas tree, O Christmas tree,
  You have a wondrous message!

Assign the following scripture passages to various members of the group. After each reading, everyone join in with the response from Psalm 96.

Reading from Genesis (Sign of the test)
And the Lord God planted a garden in Eden, in the east; and there he put the man whom he had formed. And out of the ground the Lord God made to grow every tree that is pleasant to the sight and good for food, the tree of life also in the midst of the garden, and the tree of the knowledge of good and evil. The Lord God took the man and put him in the garden of Eden to till it and keep it. And the Lord God commanded the man, saying, "You may freely eat of every tree of the garden; but of the tree of the knowledge of good and evil you shall not eat." (Gen. 2:8-9, 15-17)
Response (All)   Let the heavens be glad, and let earth rejoice,
        let the sea roar, and all that fills it;
        let the field exult, and everything in it!
      Then shall all the trees of the wood sing for joy
        before the Lord, for he comes . . .
                        (Ps. 96:11-13)

Reading from Exodus   (Sign of God's presence)
One day while Moses was taking care of the sheep and goats of his father-in-law Jethro, the priest of Midian, he led the flock across the desert and came to Sinai, the holy mountain. There the angel of the Lord appeared to him as a flame coming from the middle of a bush. Moses saw that the bush was on fire but that it was not burning up. "This is strange," he thought. "Why isn't the bush burning up? I will go closer and see." When the Lord saw that Moses was coming closer, he called to him from the middle of the bush and said, "Moses! Moses!" He answered, "Yes, here I am." God said, "Do not come any closer. Take off your sandals, because you are standing on holy ground. I am the God of your ancestors, the God of Abraham, Isaac, and Jacob." So Moses covered his face, because he was afraid to look at God. (Exod. 3:1-6 TEV)

Response   (All)

Reading from the Book of Psalms   (Sign of dedication)
> Happy are those
>   who reject the advice of evil [people,]
> who do not follow the example of sinners
>   or join those who have no use for God.
> Instead, they find joy in obeying the Law of the Lord,
>   and they study it day and night.
> They are like trees that grow beside a stream,
>   that bear fruit at the right time,
>   and whose leaves do not dry up.
> They succeed in everything they do. (Ps. 1:1-3 TEV)

Response   (All)

Reading from Isaiah   (Sign of God's concern for us)
> I will make the wilderness a pool of water,
>   and the dry land springs of water.
> I will put in the wilderness the cedar,
>   the acacia, the myrtle, and the olive;
> I will set in the desert the cypress,
>   the plane and the pine together;
> that [people] may see and know . . .
> that the hand of the Lord has done this,
>   the Holy One of Israel has created it. (Isa. 41:18-20)

Response   (All)

Reading from Matthew   (Sign of commitment)
So the disciples went and did what Jesus told them to do: they brought the donkey and the colt, threw their cloaks over them, and Jesus got on. A large crowd of people spread their cloaks on the road while others cut branches from the trees and spread them on the road. The crowds walking in front of Jesus and those walking behind began to shout, "Praise to David's Son! God bless him who comes in the name of the Lord! Praise be to God!" (Matt. 21:6-9 TEV)

Response   (All)

Reading from Luke   (Sign of integrity)
A healthy tree does not bear bad fruit, nor does a poor tree bear good fruit. Every tree is known by the fruit it bears; you do not pick figs from thorn bushes or gather grapes from bramble bushes. A good person brings good out of the treasure of good things in [the] heart; a bad person brings bad out of [a] treasure of bad things. For the mouth speaks what the heart is full of. (Luke 6:43-45 TEV)

Response   (All)

Reading from John   (Sign of life in Christ)
I am the real vine, and my Father is the gardener. He breaks off every branch in me that does not bear fruit, and he prunes every branch that does bear fruit, so that it will be clean and bear more fruit. You have been made clean already by the teaching I have given you. Remain united to me, and I will remain united to you. A branch cannot bear fruit by itself; it can do so only if it remains in the vine. In the same way you cannot bear fruit unless you remain in me. I am the vine, and you are the branches. Whoever remains in me, and I in him [or her], will bear much fruit; for you can do nothing without me. Whoever does not remain in me is thrown out like a branch and dries up; such branches are gathered up and thrown into the fire, where they are burnt. If you remain in me and my words remain in you, then you will ask for anything you wish, and you shall have it. My Father's glory is shown by your bearing much fruit; and in this way you become my disciples. (John 15:1-8 TEV)

Response   (All)

Reading from the Book of Acts   (Sign of salvation)
And when they had brought them [the apostles], they set them before the council. And the high priest questioned them, saying, "We strictly charged you not to teach in this name, yet here you have filled Jerusalem with your teaching and you intend to bring this man's blood upon us." But Peter and the apostles answered, "We must obey God rather than men. The God of our fathers raised Jesus whom you killed by hanging him on a tree. God exalted him at his right hand as Leader and Savior, to give repentance to Israel and forgiveness of sins. And we are witnesses to these things, and so is the Holy Spirit whom God has given to those who obey him." (Acts 5:27-33)

Response   (All)

Reading from the Book of Revelation   (Sign of eternal favor)
"If you have ears, then, listen to what the Spirit says to the churches! To those who win the victory I will give the right to eat the fruit of the tree of life that grows in the Garden of God." The angel also showed me the river of the water of life, sparkling like crystal, and coming from the throne of God and of the Lamb and flowing down the middle of the city's street. On each side of the river was the tree of life, which bears fruit twelve times a year, once each month; and its leaves are for the healing of the nations. (Rev. 2:7; 22:1-2 TEV)

Response   (All)

Pause for some moments of quiet reflection. Members of the group might like to share a thought or feeling or a phrase of scripture that particularly hit home.

After the reflection, let each person take a tree ornament and, beginning with the children, one by one, place the ornament on the tree, announcing as you do so, what particular gift or blessing you will ask God to give you or your family or the community or the world or those who are especially in need this Christmas.

After each person has placed an ornament and verbalized a Christmas wish, all gather around the tree as the leader collects the concerns of all in a closing prayer. You may use the following prayer, or a spontaneous one of your own, or both.

Prayer

    O good and gracious Father,
    we gather to await the fullness of hope
    symbolized by this tree.
    Grace us with your presence.
    Keep us close.
    Do not put us to the test.
    You promised to give us whatever we ask.
    Grant these requests we have dared to mention
    and those still hidden in our hearts.
    Let the leaves of this tree
    be for the healing of nations.
    Bless your people with peace and goodwill,
    through the Word-made-flesh, we pray.
    Amen.

Finish trimming the tree in a festive spirit. Serve refreshments. Sing some carols. It's a party to prepare the way of the Lord!

A Christmas Creed

Response (All)

Solemnly

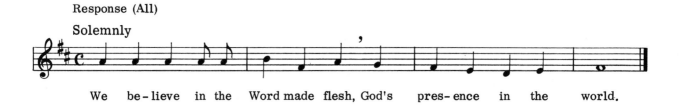

We be-lieve in the Word made flesh, God's pres-ence in the world.

We believe that in the beginning was the Word,
that the Word was with God,
that the Word was God:
that through the Word all things began;
through an outpouring of love, God created
the heavens and the earth.   *(Response)*

We believe that God touched earth,
and in a rush of tenderness
fashioned man and woman,
formed them in God's image, loving them
as a mother loves her child.   *(Response)*

We believe that God walked with us from the beginning,
in the cool of the evening and the heat of the day,
gifted us with freedom to achieve and to fail,
liberated us whenever our bondage became more than we could bear.   *(Response)*

We believe that after a long period of waiting,
the Lord of history in fact became flesh
to share our human condition:
the salt of our tears,
the thrust of our dreams,
the intensity of our loves.
We believe that he came, comes, will come again,
enlightening our darkness,
satisfying our hungers,
forgiving our sins.   *(Response)*

We believe that even now the Word is with us
and will be until the end of time.
We believe in Christ's death and resurrection
and in our own progression through death to life.
We believe in the providence of the Father
and in the Spirit's power to heal,
calling us together as one common family:
young and old, rich and poor, black and white,
oppressor and oppressed.   *(Response)*

We believe that there is hope for tomorrow
despite the discouragements of today.
For with Abraham, Isaac, and Jacob,
with the prophets and apostles,
with all of God's people,
through tests and through time
we have clung to the Promise,
and we believe
that on this night,
the Promise has been fulfilled.   *(Response)*

Solemnly

We be-lieve in the Word made flesh, God's pres-ence in the world.

Copyright © 1976 by Medical Mission Sisters, Phil., Pa.

Alternate Response (All)

In ho-ly splen-dor, be-fore the day-star, I have be-got-ten you.

Copyright © 1978 by Medical Mission Sisters, Phil., Pa.

A Birthday

Reader: In the beginning
before the mountains had been shaped
before the hills
before the beginning of the earth:
In the beginning
rejoicing
like a master workman:
In the beginning
was the Word
and the Word was with God
when God established the heavens
when God drew a circle on the face of the deep
when God marked out the foundations of the earth
the Word was with God
and the Word was God.

God said: Let there be
and there was
and it was good.
God spoke
and that voice thundered
powerful
full of majesty
breaking cedars
shaking the wilderness:
  Where were you
  when I laid the foundations of the earth
  when the morning stars sang together
  tell me
  where were you?
God spoke:
  Before I formed you in the womb
  I knew you
  I loved you with an everlasting love
  I appointed you prophet
  go and proclaim:
  thus says the Lord!
God spoke
God commanded
God called us

by our name.
God spoke
when all was in gentle silence
the Word leaped from heaven
into the midst of the land
a lamp
a light
good news
healing the brokenhearted
breathing new life into dry bones
the Word became flesh
O dry bones
and dwelt among us
dry bones
hear the Word of the Lord!

Birthday Song

Birthday Song

Thank you, God, for the gift of birth, for

love made flesh to re-fresh the earth. For

life and strength and length of days, we

give you thanks and praise.

Copyright © 1978 by Medical Mission Sisters, Phil., Pa.

(The birthday-person is invited to recite the following biblical passages. After each section, everyone repeat the birthday song.)

Lord, I put my hope in you;
I have trusted in you since I was young.
I have relied on you all my life;
you have protected me since the day I was born.
I will always praise you. (Ps. 71:5-6)
> *Repeat the song.*

Lord, you have examined me and you know me.
You know everything I do;
from far away you understand all my thoughts.

You see me, whether I am working or resting;
you know all my actions.
Even before I speak,
you already know what I will say.
You are all round me on every side;
you protect me with your power. (Ps. 139:1-5 TEV)
Repeat the song.

You created every part of me;
you put me together in my mother's womb. . . .
All you do is strange and wonderful.
I know it with all my heart.
When my bones were being formed,
carefully put together in my mother's womb,
when I was growing there in secret,
you knew that I was there—
you saw me before I was born.
The days allotted to me
had all been recorded in your book,
before any of them ever began. (Ps. 139:13-16 TEV)
Repeat the song.

Like a child that is nursed by its mother,
carried in her arms, and treated with love . . .
as tenderly as a father treats his children,
so Yahweh treats those who are fearful.
The Lord knows of what we are made,
remembers that we are dust. (Isa. 66:12 TEV; Ps. 103:13, 14*)
Repeat the song.

I will sing to the Lord as long as I live;
I will sing praise to my God while I have my being,
who fills my life with good things,
blesses me with love and mercy.
Keep me, O Lord, as the apple of your eye;
hide me in the shadow of your wings.
Give me life acording to your promise!
Give me life according to your justice!
Give me life, O Lord, according to your word!
(Ps. 104:33; 103:4, 5; 17:8; 119:154, 156, 107*)
Repeat the song.

Prayer   (By the birthday-person)
Lord, you indeed possessed me
  from the beginning of your ways.
Before you formed me in the womb,
you knew me, cherished me, chose me
  to be your very own.
For the goodness and love that surrounds me
  as long as I shall live,
I give you thanks and praise you,
  loving Father,
  tender Mother,
through Jesus Christ, your Son. Amen.

Beginning Again

We are always starting over. We are
always beginning again. Something
within us or about us changes: it is
time to be moving on. Change is seldom easy. A friendship, a favorite
spot, a familiar life-style slips
away, and nothing is the same.
May God grace all our turning points
with patience and peace.

Antiphonal reading

Alternate biblical verses and response.

Response (All)   Behold, I make all things new! (Rev. 21:5)

Verse (Leader)   The former things have passed away. (Rev. 21:4)
   Response

I am the Lord your God, . . . who leads you
 in the way you should go. (Isa. 48:17)
   Response

I myself will send an angel before you
 to guard you as you go
 and bring you to the place that
 I have prepared. (Exod. 23:20 JB)
   Response

I will go before you and level the
 mountains. (Isa. 45:2)
   Response

I will turn the darkness before [you] into light, the
 rough places into level ground. (Isa. 42:16)
   Response

Do not let your hearts be troubled.
Trust in God still, and trust in me. (John 14:1 JB)
   Response

The following fragment from Paul's letter to the community at Philippi is rich with meaning when shared prior to the parting of friends.

Reading   I thank my God whenever I think of you; and every time I pray for all of you,
I pray with joy, remembering how you have helped to spread the Good News
from the day you first heard it right up to the present. I am quite certain that

the One who began this good work in you will see that it is finished when the Day of Christ Jesus comes. It is only natural that I should feel like this towards you all, since you have shared the privileges which have been mine: both my chains and my work defending and establishing the gospel. You have a permanent place in my heart, and God knows how much I miss you all, loving you as Christ Jesus loves you.

If our life in Christ means anything to you, if love can persuade at all, or the Spirit that we have in common, or any tenderness and sympathy, then be united in your convictions and united in your love, with a common purpose and a common mind.

Do not give way but remain faithful in the Lord. I miss you very much, dear friends; you are my joy and my crown.

(Phil. 1:3-8; 2:1-2; 4:1 JB)

Antiphonal reading

Alternate biblical verses and response.

Response (All)   Goodness and mercy shall follow me
       all the days of my life. (Ps. 23:6)

Verse (Leader)   Yahweh said to Abram, "Leave your country,
       your family, and your father's house, for
       the land I will show you." (Gen. 12:1 JB)
          Response

Bless the Lord God on every occasion; ask . . .
       that your ways may be made straight and that
       all your paths and plans may prosper. (Tob. 4:19)
          Response

Accept whatever is brought upon you, and in
       changes that humble you be patient. For
       gold is tested in the fire. (Sir. 2:4-5)
          Response

The beloved of the Lord . . . dwells in safety.
The eternal God is your dwelling place, and
       underneath are the everlasting arms. (Deut. 33:12, 27)
          Response

Time of silence, shared prayer
    Members of the group might wish to verbalize prayers for the present, hopes for the future, or cherished moments for remembering.

Closing Prayer
    God, loving Father,
    there is nothing that can separate us
       from your providence
       or the love of Christ Jesus, your Son.
    Seasons pass, times change,
    your care of us remains,
    transparent now and often
       in the strong, supportive love of friends.
    With your tender mercy, visit us,
       to guide our feet in the way of peace.
    Guard our lives,
       our going and coming,
       now and forever. Amen.

An appropriate song: "Long Road to Freedom" (from the album *Joy Is Like the Rain* by the Medical Mission Sisters)

2053992

Turning Points

Time
turns
taking us
where we would not choose to go.
Suddenly we pass a point
we will never pass again.
Turning points interrupt us—
there must be some mistake!
Looking back we see them
for what they really are:
bittersweet raw reality
breakthrough to beatitude
bedrock that gives us courage
to give ourselves away.
The less we struggle with turning points
the greater the strength remaining
to return
and turn
again.

Deserts

When our lives are fruitful
our environment enriching
inner resources sources of growth,
the desert doesn't scare us.
Beware! It overtakes those
who litter love with the blanched
and brittle bones of their discontent.
Dreams disintegrate, hope dries up,
parched spirits thirst for Living Water,
scratch deceptive surfaces
in search of hidden springs.
Deserts are barren burial grounds
or gardens where the living God
speaks to the listening heart.

Reading When my people in their need look for water,
when their throats are dry with thirst,
then I, the Lord, will answer their prayer;
I, the God of Israel, will never abandon them.
I will make rivers flow among barren hills
and springs of water run in the valleys.
I will turn the desert into pools of water
and the dry land into flowing springs.

I will give water to the thirsty land
and make streams flow on the dry ground.
I will pour out my power on your children
and my blessing on your descendants.
They will thrive like well-watered grass,
like willows by streams of running water. (Isa. 41:17-18; 44:3-4 TEV)

Antiphonal recitation
> *Alternate the following verses of Psalm 107 between two people or two groups, adding the response at the beginning and end, or let one person do the reading and the rest respond after every verse.*

Response (All) If anyone is thirsty, come to me and drink. (John 7:37*)

Verses O give thanks to the Lord who is good,
whose steadfast love endures for ever!

Let the redeemed of the Lord say so,
those whom the Lord has redeemed from trouble
and gathered in from the lands.

Some wandered in desert wastes,
finding no way to a city to dwell in;
hungry and thirsty, their soul fainted within them.

They cried to the Lord in their trouble,
and the Lord delivered them from their distress;
the Lord led them by a straight way,
till they reached a city to dwell in.

Let them thank the Lord for such steadfast love,
for such wonderful works to those in need,
satisfying all who are thirsty,
filling the hungry with good things.

The Lord turns a desert into pools of water,
a parched land into springs.
There the hungry dwell
and establish a city to live in,
sow fields, plant vineyards,
and get a fruitful yield.

Whoever is wise, give heed to these things;
let everyone consider
the steadfast love of the Lord.

Response (All)   If anyone is thirsty, come to me and drink.
Song "Living Water"
A song for enroute or on arrival, for young or old, up or down, for formal praying, informal playing, for born-again occasions, fellowship and fun.

Living Water

Words and music by
Sister Miriam Therese Winter

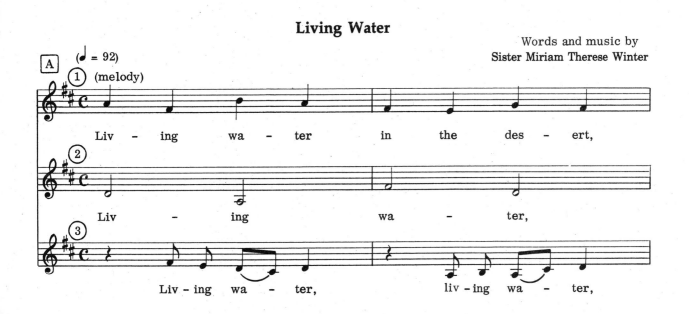

in the des - ert, hard to find. Liv - ing wa - ter,

cool and kind. Heal my

liv - ing__ wa - ter, cool and kind. Heal - ing__ wa - ter,

wash the des - ert, wash the des - ert of my mind.

heart and mend my mind.

heal - ing__ wa - ter, heal - ing wa - ter, heal__ my__ mind.

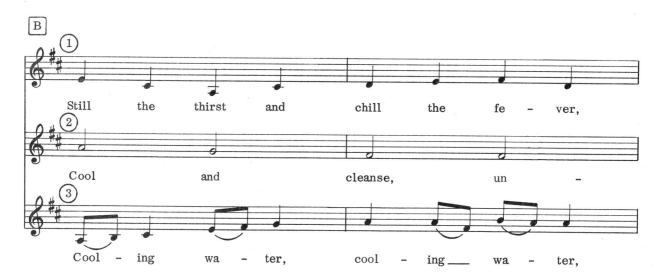

B

① Still the thirst and chill the fe - ver,

② Cool and cleanse, un -

③ Cool - ing wa - ter, cool - ing__ wa - ter,

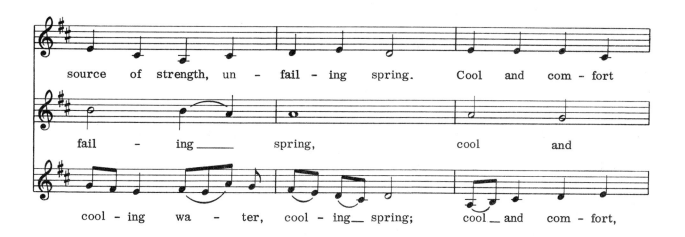

source of strength, un - fail - ing spring. Cool and com - fort

fail - ing _____ spring, cool and

cool - ing wa - ter, cool - ing_ spring; cool _ and com - fort,

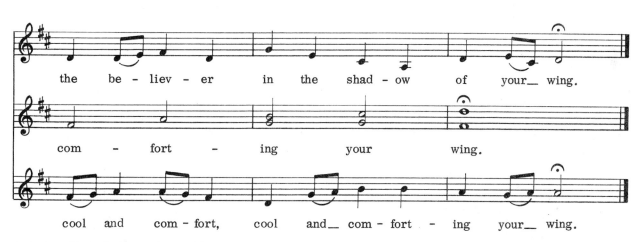

the be - liev - er in the shad - ow of your_ wing.

com - fort - ing your wing.

cool and com - fort, cool and_ com - fort - ing your_ wing.

© MCMLXXVI by Medical Mission Sisters, Phil., Pa. Reprinted by permission Vanguard Music Corp., 250 W. 57th St.,
N.Y., N.Y. 10019

"Living Water" is a song for deserts and oases,
for the heart that is parched and empty,
for the spirit spilling over with joy.
Sing the song simply, in unison,
or add ② for a two-part harmony,
even ③, if the group is able,
and let its rippling tones heal your heart.

Hunger

Today the whole world hungers:
for food, freedom and justice,
understanding and truth, peace,
for the Father, the Spirit,
the Bread of Life.
Our hunger for good arises
from a deep-rooted hunger
for God.

The following does not necessarily constitute a prayer service design, although it may be used as such. The purpose of the pieces gathered here is to alert us to the crisis of hunger within the human family. Hopefully a growing awareness will lead to an active, effective concern. These elements may be used in a variety of ways at various times and places. Use one or several or all of them as part of your consciousness-raising prayer.

Reflection One

To be human is to be hungry. Not to be hungry is to be dead. Yet in our contemporary way of life, many peoples of the world—including almost all the Christians—have such a high standard of living that they (we) have long forgotten about hunger. In our technically oriented society, we frequently think of ourselves more or less as machines. Mealtimes come, and we refuel. Our hunger is satisfied so quickly, so easily, so continuously, that we can easily forget that hunger is there at all; it does not intrude itself. There is one obvious disadvantage to this. One who is never hungry is unlikely to have compassion or concern for those who are constantly hungry and never satisfied.

To be hungry is to experience oneself as insufficient, as having needs, as being unable to guarantee one's own existence. To be hungry is to know in a dark, inchoate kind of way that we do not create ourselves but receive our existence as a gift. Never to be hungry is to be in danger of forgetting reverence and gratitude to the source of our being—the transcendent Creator. It is not by accident that eating, side by side with birth and death, has always been a central occasion for human communities to pray.

Hunger also brings into focus our dependence on others. We eat bread sliced for us by one person, bought from another, transported by another, baked by yet another with flour ground by still others from grain grown in fields cultivated with machinery made by others from metal extracted from the earth by others again. We who are habitually well-fed are in danger of forgetting this interdependence and living as though we had produced our own food just because we have earned a cash salary—or received dividends on an investment we never earned. Those who are habitually hungry are ever mindful of this interdependence. They know that their lives are hostages in others' hands—not only their sheer survival but the quality of their lives, the extent of their freedom to be human.

Hunger has many meanings. The basic physical hunger for food has very close analogies in the needs that people have for other kinds of sustenance far less easily recognized and identified. Basic hunger quickly broadens into the need for physical sustenance more generally—the need for warmth, cover, rest, clean air, and so on. But equally pervasive, equally important, and far more subtle is the need to be loved into being and the hunger in which that need manifests itself. The experience of that need and that hunger is a general experience common to all persons.

The deep, deep need that each of us has to be called forth into the fullness of being of creative love often makes itself felt in a hunger to be worthwhile, to be valued or appreciated, to have a purpose or goal in life. It has been observed that, in the contemporary world, those who most insistently complain of finding that hunger unfulfilled are also those who individually or collectively are amassing and hoarding and wasting so much of the material resources of the world that others are kept on the verge of starvation.

It is worth some reflection to try to discern the patterns of this self-maintaining cycle of human suffering. For a person who feels unvalued, unappreciated, and goalless is not capable of generosity and appreciation of others and therefore, not capable of empathy and concern with their hunger and their need. In the strictest sense, such a person needs to be rescued, redeemed, or saved as much as the starving person whose quality of life is shriveled and brutalized needs to be rescued, redeemed, or saved. Both are living a life that is unfree, less than human, and marred by needless suffering. But the fearful frustration and torture of the physically starving person can only be resolved by that redemption of the love-starved which consists of a radical conversion from self-centeredness to engagement with and for others.

Our most urgent need is to unmask the real hunger behind the frantic quest for possessions and buying power on the part of those who already have a disproportionately large share of these—the real hunger behind the sense of insecurity that powers the arms race and the huge defense expenditures of the strongest nations. Beyond the unmasking of the real hunger, we are in need of a process of conversion from cramped, defensive selfishness to an outward focus—a process of conversion not only for individuals but for groups, organizations, and institutions ranging from families to nations.

So much of the suffering in the world comes not from natural disaster but from human behavior, and so much of the human behavior that causes the suffering is motivated by considerations of self-defense and self-preservation that have slid out of focus. (Monika Hellwig, *The Eucharist and the Hunger of the World*)

Reflection Two

Hunger is
when someone you love leaves
you empty
       leaves
locking the door
         leaves
you standing wide
with wants unsatisfied

is
when you walk small beside
a savage sea
when your need to give goes wild
when you wake
writhing
and find you are not
with child.

Reflection Three

If I experience such hunger
there must be bread
somewhere
with which I can be fed.
If I burn so fiercely
there must be stick
or tallow
to feed my flaming wick.
If I am so utterly empty
God must have willed
Someone
with whom I can be filled.
Hunger, heat, emptiness
drive me to demand
food
wood
substance
from that fulfilling hand.
As I devour life
I am consumed.
Resurrection: rifle
the entombed.

Reflection Four—God's Word
   *The following scriptural passages have been selected and compiled to dramatize our dependency
on God and one another for that promised daily bread. This reflection invites the participation of
five individual readers: the Narrator (N), the Lord (1), humanity in general (2), specific human
voices (3), (4), as well as the entire group (All).*

N: Thus says the Lord:

1: If you walk in my ways and observe my commandments
     and do them, then I will give you your rains in their
     due season, and the land shall yield its increase,
     and the trees of the field shall yield their fruit.
     And your threshing shall last to the time of vintage,
     and the vintage shall last to the time of sowing;
     and you shall eat your bread to the full,
     and dwell in your land securely . . .
     and I will walk among you, and will be your God,
     and you shall be my people. (Lev. 26:3-6, 12)

2: You shall eat and be full,
     and you shall bless the Lord your God
     for the good land [the Lord] has given you. (Deut. 8:10)

1: Come, eat of my bread.
2: Come, eat of my bread.
All: Come, eat of my bread. (Prov. 9:5)

1: Everyone who thirsts, come to the waters;
. . . who has no money, come, buy and eat. (Isa. 55:1*)
You shall eat in plenty and be satisfied,
and praise the name of the Lord your God. (Joel 2:26)

2: Bring forth food from the earth,
and wine to gladden the heart,
oil to make the face shine,
and bread to strengthen the heart. (Ps. 104:14-15*)
Honor the Lord with your substance
and with the first fruits of all your produce;
then your barns will be filled with plenty,
and your vats will be bursting with wine. (Prov. 3:9-10)

1: Come, eat of my bread.
2: Come, eat of my bread.
All: Come, eat of my bread.

2: All living things look hopefully to you
and you give them food when they need it. (Ps. 145:15-16 TEV)

3: You have sown much, and harvested little;
4: you eat, but you never have enough;
3: you drink, but you never have your fill;
4: you clothe yourselves, but no one is warm.

3: Therefore the heavens above you have withheld the dew,
4: and the earth has withheld its produce (Hag. 1:6, 10)

N: More than 460 million people are permanently hungry.
The majority of these are threatened by starvation.☆
All: Give us this day our daily bread. (Matt. 6:11)

N: More than ten million people—most of them under five years of age—will perish
this year as a result of too little food.☆
All: Give us this day our daily bread.

N: The problem is not that there is not enough food to go around. The problem is that
enough food does not get around.☆
All: Give us this day our daily bread.

3: All her people groan as they search for bread;
4: they trade their treasures for food to revive their strength.
3: "Look, O Lord, and behold, for I am despised."
4: "Is it nothing to you, all you who pass by?
Look and see if there is any sorrow like my sorrow." (Lam. 1:11-12)

3: What [one] of you, if [your] son ask [you] for bread, will give him a stone?
4: Or if he asks for fish, will give him a serpent? (Matt. 7:9-10)

N: Every man, woman and child has the inalienable right to be free from hunger.☆
N: Every man, woman and child has the inalienable right to be free from hunger.☆
All: Share your bread with the hungry. (Isa. 58:7)

N: We must produce enough food for every human being on earth—and we can!☆

      All: Share your bread with the hungry.

N: We must realize that all nations are interdependent and use our resources for mutual benefit—and we can!☆

      All: Share your bread with the hungry.

N: Thus says the Lord:

1: Blessed are you that hunger now,
for you shall be satisfied.
Woe to you that are full now,
for you shall hunger. (Luke 6:21, 25)

2: The Lord fills the hungry with good things
    and sends the rich away empty. (Luke 1:53*)

N: Thus says the Lord:

1: Behold, my servants shall eat, but you shall be hungry;
behold, my servants shall drink, but you shall be thirsty;
behold, my servants shall rejoice, but you shall be
    put to shame.
For behold, I create new heavens and a new earth;
and the former things shall not be remembered. (Isa. 65:13, 17)

N: Thus says the Lord:

1: "Come, you that are blessed by my Father! Come and possess the kingdom which has been prepared for you ever since the creation of the world. I was hungry and you fed me, thirsty and you gave me a drink; I was a stranger and you received me in your homes, naked and you clothed me; I was sick and you took care of me, in prison and you visited me."

N: The righteous will then answer him:

2: "When, Lord, did we ever see you hungry and feed you, or thirsty and give you drink? When did we see you a stranger and welcome you in our homes, or naked and clothe you? When did we see you sick or in prison, and visit you?"

N: The King will reply:
1: "I tell you, whenever you did this for one of the least important of these brothers [and sisters] of mine, you did it for me!" (Matt. 25:34-41 TEV)

N: Thus says the Lord:

1: Give, and it will be given to you; good measure,
pressed down, shaken together, running over,
will be put into your lap. For the measure you give
will be the measure you get back. (Luke 6:38)

Song "Heavenly Father"

Note: The lines marked with a star (☆) are not from Scripture. They are contemporary statistics.

You might try adding a visual dimension to the above scriptural reflection. The rich imagery of the verses suggests a wide variety of pictures. The contrast of need and abundance is all the more unforgettable when it bombards the eye. Borrow, buy, or make your own Instamatic or 35mm slides. Simplify the reading to one or two voices alternating parts.

Heavenly Father

Words and music by
Sister Miriam Therese Winter

© MCMLXXVI by Medical Mission Sisters, Phil., Pa. Reprinted by permission Vanguard Music Corp., 250 W. 57th St.,
N.Y., N.Y. 10019

We must come to terms with hunger,
with the brutal fact that most of the world
goes hungry every day
while what we waste would satisfy
so many wasted lives.
The first step is awareness.
The second is to act.

Prayers to Heighten Awareness
Copy out the following prayers and carry them in your pocket. Pray them aloud. Pass them
around. Maybe when all our hungers are linked into one unbearable ache, maybe then we will
share resources, unselfishly mete out justice, and break the bread of peace.

(Monday) *Hunger for Food*
Give us this day we beg, O God,
sufficient daily bread.
Free your people from famine,
destitution, drought,
from a selfish misuse of resources,
from wastefulness and want.
Give us enough
and more than enough.
Give us the grace to share.
Satisfy all who hunger for food
with good things in abundance,
pressed down, running over,
today, tomorrow, and every day
until you come again. Amen.

(Tuesday) *Hunger for Freedom and Justice*
Deliver us from evil, Lord:
pollution, persecution,
violence, false values,
ingratitude, and greed.
Break those bonds that keep us
from bearing another's burden,
from being brother, sister, neighbor
to anyone in need.
Prisoners, we imprison.
Impoverished, we make others poor.
Oppressed, so we oppress.
We hunger for freedom, for justice.
Liberate us! Amen.

(Wednesday) *Hunger for Understanding and Truth*
Gracious God, teach us to trust
what we do not understand.
So much senseless suffering,
so much spoiled potential,
such a lack of meaning
meets us at every turn.
Faith means
still believing
in the midst of our unbelief

that in you there is understanding,
you alone are the truth
for which we hunger. Amen.

(Thursday) *Hunger for Peace*
Forgive us, Lord, for all the times
our hearts have gone to war,
for hatreds nurtured,
wounds inflicted,
damages already done.
Help us make peace
in fulfillment of the promises you gave us,
with family, friends,
neighbor, nation,
and right around the globe.
God of peace, be with us all
who hunger for peace. Amen.

(Friday) *Hunger for the Father*
Remember us, our Father.
We are that new creation
you once called forth from clay:
reborn, redeemed, revisited,
reflecting the very image
of your saving word and deed.
We hunger now to know you well,
to experience your nearness
in these intensely troubled times.
May all be one,
your will be done,
throughout the earth. Amen.

(Saturday) *Hunger for the Spirit*
Spirit of God, you are the bond
of everlasting love,
our longing for love, for friendship,
for relationships that last.
For this little while
empower us
with the impact of your presence.
We hunger for you, gift-giving Spirit
of love, of life. Amen.

(Sunday) *Hunger for the Bread of Life*
Jesus, you are the Bread of Life,
bread broken
in order to mend all
broken dreams,
broken people,
broken homes and hearts.
Break the good news gently
to suffering, struggling spirits,
that you are nourishment to anyone
who hungers for life. Amen.

47

Action
Awareness should lead to serious concern and a growing desire to act. Design a program of action for your family, church, or group. There are many possibilities from which to choose. Plan on having a simple meal, such as soup and bread. Give the money you save toward a local need, or send it to an organization that will use it effectively abroad (for instance, BREAD FOR THE WORLD, 235 East 49th Street, New York, New York 10017). This action would be an appropriate link to the ancient Lenten fast. Do it weekly during Lent and continue it monthly throughout the year, for some evils can only be overcome by prayer and fasting. Or collect canned goods for those who need it. Or prepare and serve a meal at a hospice that helps the down-and-out. Or visit a shut-in, or the elderly, who hunger for companionship. Perhaps your own family or community craves more of your time and talent. Hunger is all around us. Are we discerning enough, motivated enough, to do something about it?

A Table Prayer
The following grace before meals is a reminder to be grateful for what we have been given. We have a responsibility never to forget the multitudes who are in need.

Grace Before a Meal
Generous God,
bless this food
we gratefully bring before you.
May it be for us and for all your people
sign and symbol of sustenance
throughout this hungry earth.
May crops increase and multiply.
May there be enough, more than enough,
for all to eat their fill.
As we share the food our bodies crave,
satisfy our deeper hunger
to break the Bread of Life.
Nourish us now
and every day
forever and ever. Amen.

Questions

This prayer requires preparation. Each participant is asked to gather at least three scriptural questions. Throughout the Bible there are questions that people have addressed to God, or to one another concerning God, or that God addresses to us. The aim here is to experience that our faith is a faith full of questions. Select one question from the Old Testament, one from the Gospels, one from the remaining New Testament books . . . or assign each person a different book . . . or leave everything up to chance. This task can be done in advance so that people come together with their questions already in hand. Or spend the first fifteen minutes separately, searching the scriptures in silence. Be sure then that you provide enough Bibles for all.

Begin by gathering in a circle. Light a candle if it helps the mood. Savor being still.

Leader:
> We are so sure, so certain,
> about everything, even God.
> We seldom dare to question.
> We rarely admit to doubt.
> Yet the ways of the Lord are mystery.
> Who really understands?
> We turn to you for guidance, God.
> We who have all the answers
> now listen to your Word.

Time of Sharing

Invite the group to share prayerfully, at random, one at a time, the scriptural questions they have brought. Perhaps in the presence of the Spirit, these will resonate with those questions lurking in the secrecy of our hearts.

You might begin with one of the following questions, just to get things started, interspersing the others from time to time. Whether the group numbers 5, 55, or 105, the questions are usually varied. Some are sure to hit home.

+ Am I my brother's keeper? (Gen. 4:9)
+ How long must I bear pain in my soul, and have sorrow in my heart all the day? (Ps. 13:2)
+ Who are you, Lord? (Acts 9:5)
+ What sign will you give to show us that we should believe in you? (John 6:30 JB)
+ How can a grown man be born? Can he go back into his mother's womb and be born again? (John 3:4-5 JB)
+ What is truth? (John 18:38)
+ Who is the greatest in the kingdom of heaven? (Matt. 18:1)
+ Who is my neighbor? (Luke 10:29)
+ What about us? . . . We have left everything and followed you. (Mark 10:28 JB)
+ In that case . . . who can be saved? (Mark 10:26 JB)
+ Master, do you not care? We are going down! (Mark 4:38 JB)

When the time of sharing is finished, the leader sums up the experience with the following prayer-reflection.

Prayer-Reflection

We thank you, Father, for the insight and the comfort
of your Word. We are grateful to discover
that our faith is full of questions,
that you were questioned often
even by your best friends:

Abraham mocked: "Is a child to be born to a man one hundred years old?" (Gen. 17:17)

Moses: "Who am I to go to Pharaoh?" (Exod. 3:11) and the questions of all the prophets uncertain of their call . . .

Jonah: How dare God salvage Nineveh after he had announced its doom!

Job: Why me? . . . and Mary: "How can this be, for I have no knowledge of man?" (Luke 1:34)

John: "Are you the one who is to come or have we to wait for someone else? (Luke 7:20)

Jesus himself: as a child, daring to question the rabbis . . . daring to question his Father: "My God, my God, why have you abandoned me?" (Mark 15:34)

Help us, Lord, to live with questions, to cope with the ambiguities that permeate our lives. You alone are the answer, revealed to us bit by bit. We praise you, Known and Unknown, and go forward in faith. Amen.

Benediction   Be patient toward all that is unsolved in your heart . . . try to love the questions themselves like locked rooms and like books written in a very foreign tongue. Do not now seek the answers, which cannot be given you because you would not be able to live them. And the point is, to live everything. Live the questions now. Perhaps you will then gradually, without noticing it, live along some distant day into the answer.
(Rainer Maria Rilke)

Night

Song   "Long Is Our Winter" (from the album *Grailville Sings*)

What do you do when the light goes out,
when darkness overtakes you,
and you don't know where to turn?
Are you suddenly more loving?
Or desperately afraid?
Does every single sorrow
send you toward despair,
or can you see it as "shade of his hand
outstretched caressingly"?
Night holds a promise of morning.
That's why God made stars.

After reading the preceding passage, plunge the room into darkness, and wait. When it seems time to continue, light a candle and select one, or several, of the following poems to be read reflectively. After an appropriate pause, proclaim the scripture passage as counterpoint, then sit silently together as each gets in touch with his or her own darkness. Close singing "Night."
Some Poems

A   Will it be long
or always
this midnight
where few stars shine?
Will you for long be storm
my Christ
and thunder
under my eaves
jarring my windows?
This wind heaves
the fine edge of my desires
beyond my reach.
Or will each flash
across my night
sear my sight and light
my blindness
with gentle warning:
before so very long it will be
 morning.

Dawn rips the flesh of night.

51

B Light pours from its open wound
and we rejoice.
Your voice, O Christ,
pierces my night.
My heart balks and bleeds,
baring my most fundamental needs.
Growth demands
a rupture.
                    Only the poor
of spirit
lift sore souls to the sword's point
and endure.

C In the deep
in the deep dark
in the deep dread dark
of late fall
much happens
underneath
the frenzy of all
that wind.
Listen
to how the whole world listens
waits
watches
contemplates.
Friends of God
at pains to sing
hear strains of far-off banqueting
see certain signs
of wine-bowls brimmed
make haste to assure that all their lamps
are trimmed.

With head held high

D against the eastern rim of sky,
Ezekiel's gate stood barred
to every transitory thing,
dropped its guard but seldom:
gave entrance to the King.
Mary, the dawn,
stood on the very brink of night
when Morning came.
                    Light
broke upon her softly
as Christ the Key encountered virgin latch.
Life lay in wait
until the Sun passed through its eastern gate.
Then joy! Then song!
Time had been long, been lonely.
Now we know every day as Easter only.

Scripture Human life is like forced army service,
like a life of hard manual labor,
like a slave longing for the cool shade;
like a worker waiting for his pay.
Month after month I have nothing to live for;
Night after night brings me grief.
When I lie down to sleep, the hours drag;
I toss all night and long for dawn. (Job 7:1-4 TEV)
Listen, O Lord, to my plea for justice;
pay attention to my cry for help!
You know my heart. You have come to me at night;
you have examined me completely
and found no evil desire in me.
Protect me as you would your very eyes;
hide me in the shadow of your wings. (Ps. 17:1, 3, 8 TEV)
Silent Reflection
Song   "Night"   (from the album *Knock, Knock,* by the Medical
Mission Sisters)

Night

Words and music by
Sister Miriam Therese Winter

With feeling (♩ = 72)

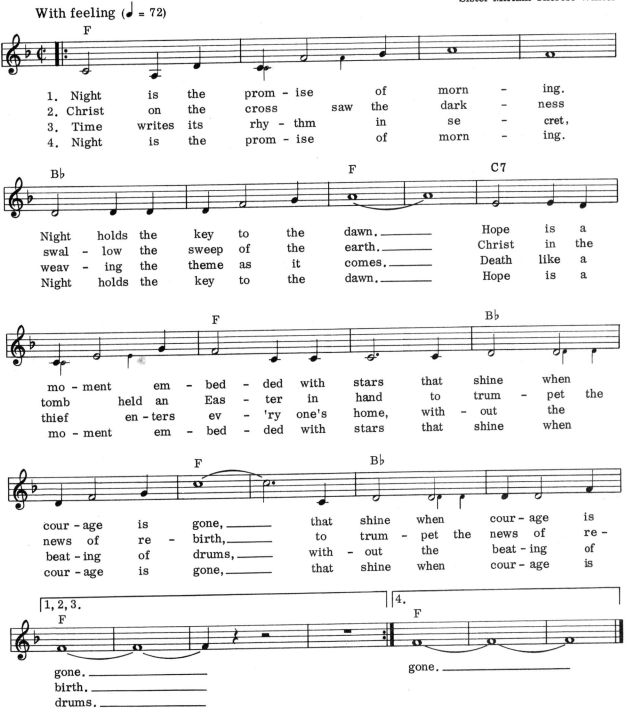

1. Night is the prom - ise of morn - ing.
2. Christ on the cross saw the dark - ness
3. Time writes its rhy - thm in se - cret,
4. Night is the prom - ise of morn - ing.

Night holds the key to the dawn. _____ Hope is a
swal - low the sweep of the earth. _____ Christ in the
weav - ing the theme as it comes. _____ Death like a
Night holds the key to the dawn. _____ Hope is a

mo - ment em - bed - ded with stars that shine when
tomb held an Eas - ter in hand to trum - pet the
thief en - ters ev - 'ry one's home, with - out the
mo - ment em - bed - ded with stars that shine when

cour - age is gone, _____ that shine when cour - age is
news of re - birth, _____ to trum - pet the news of re -
beat - ing of drums, _____ with - out the beat - ing of
cour - age is gone, _____ that shine when cour - age is

[1, 2, 3.]

gone. _____
birth. _____
drums. _____

[4.]

gone. _____

© MCMLXVIII by Medical Mission Sisters, Phil., Pa. Reprinted by permission Vanguard Music Corp., 250 W. 57th St.,
N.Y., N.Y. 10019

Long Is Our Winter

Words by Eleanor Walker

German folk melody

Transcription from the recording, "Grailville Sings: Music of Advent and Christmas."

Paradox

        Father,
we have come to call this Friday "Good."
This day of whipping, stumbling, plotting,
    nails and tears
    and determined mindless missing of the point.
This day on which your Son is hated to death.
This day on which your Word is pinned up against the sky
    and silenced.
This day on which prophecies have their moment of truth,
    and in the incredible desolation
        of the after-noon Calvary
    some are indeed heard to say,
    "My God, he must have been the one. . . . "
We have come to call this Friday "Good."
We come, Father, and ask once more the grace of retrospect
    as we sit again at the feet
        of this specific darkness

                    pain

                    absurdity

                    failure

                    lack of power

            and last-breathing.

We ask to absorb the day's darknesses,
    knowing them in our many selves.
We need to gently, but again,
    sense ourselves and times

        as whipper

            stumbler

            plotter

            nailer and nailed.

We need to know the broken Lord
    in these our heres and nows.

55

We have come to call this Friday "Good."
And it is perhaps because
  it is salutary for us
  to know again . . . again . . .
    that your Son stood still for death
    because only in the utter completeness
      of that anguished handing over
    could the word *life*
    could the word *peace*
    could the words *whole* and *heal*
      be renamed in truth.
Which is to say redeemed.
Father, we have come to call this Friday "Good."
Absorb us in your silent sense of it.
Grace us with its goodness. Amen.
                              (Loretta Whalen)

Second Movement

Refrain (All) Our Shepherd, fountain of living water, is gone.

Leader A voice was heard in Ramah . . . Rachel weeping for her children, refusing to be comforted because they were no more. (Matt. 2:18 JB)

Refrain

Surely the bridegroom's attendants would never think of mourning as long as the bridegroom is still with them? But the time will come for the bridegroom to be taken away from them, and then they will fast. (Matt. 9:15 JB)

Refrain

As Jonah was in the belly of the sea-monster for three days and three nights, so will the Son of Man be in the heart of the earth for three days and three nights. (Matt. 12:40 JB)

Refrain

The Son of Man is going to be handed over into the power of men; they will put him to death, and on the third day he will be raised to life again. (Matt. 17:22 JB)

Refrain

Jerusalem, Jerusalem, you that kill the prophets and stone those who are sent to you. You shall not see me any more until you say: *Blessings on him who comes in the name of the Lord!* (Matt. 23:37, 39 JB)

Refrain

You will look for me and will not find me: where I am you cannot come. (John 7:34 JB)

Refrain

I am the good shepherd . . . and I lay down my life for my sheep. (John 10:14-15 JB)

Refrain

He was pierced through for our faults, crushed for our sins. His soul's anguish over, he shall see the light and be content. (Isa. 53:5, 11 JB)

Refrain

The light will be with you only a little longer now.
Walk while you have the light. (John 12:35 JB)

Refrain

After I have gone and prepared you a place, I shall return to take you with me; so that where I am you may be too. (John 14:3 JB)

Refrain

Do not let your hearts be troubled or afraid. You heard me say: I am going away, and shall return. (John 14:27-28 JB)
Refrain
I will not leave you orphans; I will come back to you. (John 14:18 JB)
Refrain

First Voice: Father,
our shepherd, fountain of living water,
is gone.
Gone, the force that gave life meaning.
Gone, anything of consequence.
Gone, all but the bitter thought:
we brought it on ourselves.
They have taken our life away,
and we don't know where to find it.

How often we kill the thing we love
by leaving it
    losing it
    loving it to death.
Death allows no second chance.
Usually.
But once, once beyond a time
our wildest wish came true,
and you rewrote the story line as
happy ever after.

We grapple again with that interim
of emptiness
    absence
    sense of loss
that we might recall how close we came
to throwing it all away,
how dangerously close we still come
to missing the point.
This little while
    —is it?
or will there be a long, long pause
until you come again?

Our fountain of living water
is gone.
Our Father,
into your hands we commend our thirst,
into your hands our spirit, your Son,
into your hands, our Father.
Forgive us.
Your will be done. Amen.

Second Voice:
Wait
but one day more
the door of death will dangle
useless
as light, laughter, song long-silenced

57

bellows to the sky:
I have borne your burden
I have heard your cry
Then night will reign more glorious than day,
and Christ will wipe one worry more
away.

Third Movement
The bittersweet paradox of death-to-life
is our central turning point,
that profound breakthrough enabling us
to prioritize again.
Some things are best said in song.
Augustine had the right idea.
Who loves more than he or she can say,
sings! he said;
and then went one step further:
The one who sings, prays twice!
Come, then.
Catch a glimpse of Easter
through these songs.

What follows is one moment in that memorable night of nights. Congregations observing the traditional Vigil Service will find the following settings of the Exsultet, Great Preface, and Triple Alleluia appropriate for liturgical use. Others might like to incorporate them, whole or in part, into their sunrise service, or simply sing them "just because."

Response for the Procession of Lights

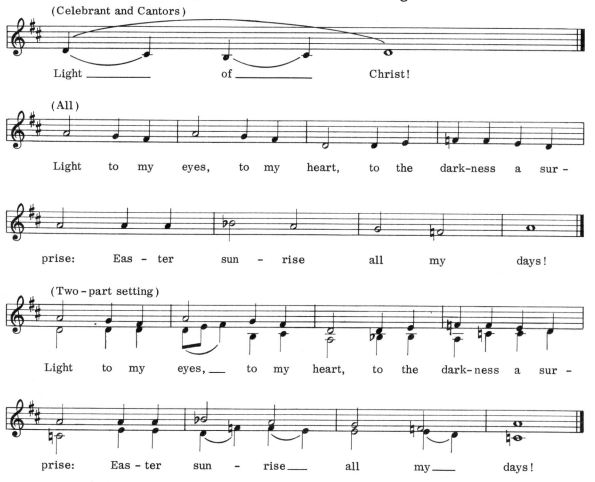

Copyright © 1976 by Medical Mission Sisters, Phil., Pa.

Rejoice Now!

Words and music
beginning line 4 by
Sister Miriam Therese Winter

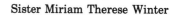

Cantor

Re - joice___ now, all you heav - en - ly choirs of an - gels. Re - joice___

all cre - a - tion a - round His throne, for this might - y King is

vic - to - ri - ous. Sound,___ O trum - pet, tell of our sal - va - tion.

Choir

G/   C/   G/   F♯m/   D7/

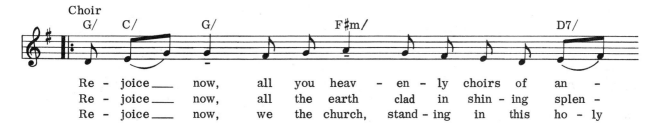

Re - joice_____ now, all you heav - en - ly choirs of an -
Re - joice_____ now, all the earth clad in shin - ing splen -
Re - joice_____ now, we the church, stand - ing in this ho - ly

G   All   Bm   Am

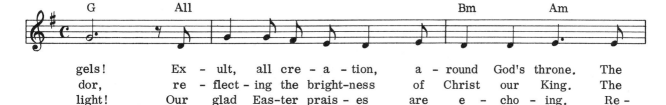

gels!   Ex - ult, all cre - a - tion, a - round God's throne. The
dor,   re - flect - ing the bright-ness of Christ our King. The
light!   Our glad Eas-ter prais - es are e - cho - ing. Re -

G   G

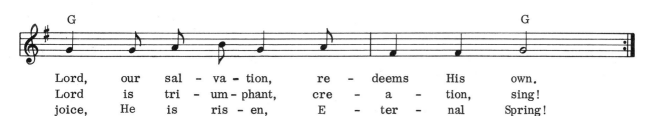

Lord, our sal - va - tion, re - deems His own.
Lord is tri - um - phant, cre - a - tion, sing!
joice, He is ris - en, E - ter - nal Spring!

© MCMLXXVI by Medical Mission Sisters, Phil., Pa. Reprinted by permission Vanguard Music Corp., 250 W. 57th St., N.Y., N.Y. 10019

This Is the Night

Solemn Preface of Easter

This is the night when God delivered our forefathers
    from their chains,
led them dry-shod through the sea, out of slavery.
Free your people once again.
This is the night when Christ has ransomed us and paid
    the price of sin.
The Paschal Lamb was slain, bringing peace through pain.
We will follow where he's been.
This is the night. This is the night he rose triumphant
    from the grave,
opened what was sealed, forgave and blessed and healed
those he suffered death to save.
O happy fault! O necessary sin!
A New Day rushes in!

This is the night the pillar of fire becomes a beacon
    of belief
to lead the people on, when hope is nearly gone,
unwavering joy consuming grief.
This is the night. This is the night of nights most blessed
    since time began,
when death is our rebirth, with heaven wed to earth.
Praise God's reconciling plan!
This is the night. This is the night of joy,
    of solemn songs of praise,
washing guilt away. The night shall be as day,
mourning turned to dancing all our days.
O happy fault! O necessary sin!
A New Day rushes in!

©MCMLXXVI by Medical Mission Sisters, Phil., Pa. Reprinted by permission Vanguard Music Corp., 250 W. 57th St., N.Y., N.Y. 10019

Triple Alleluia

+ State the first Alleluia on a flute or an organ flute stop. The congregation then repeats that Alleluia *a capella.*

+ Follow the same procedure for the second Alleluia.

+ Approach the third Alleluia the same way, adding the full accompaniment of guitars and/or organ to the congregation's song.

Al - le - lu - ia.

Al - le - lu - ia.

Al - le - lu - ia.

Copyright © 1976 by Medical Mission Sisters, Phil., Pa.

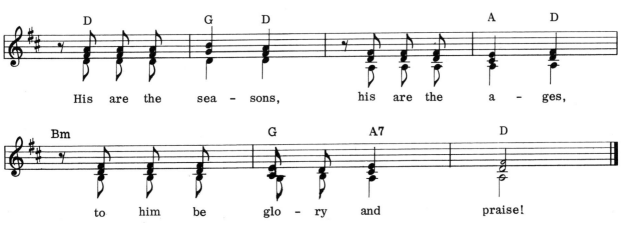

His are the sea - sons, his are the a - ges,

to him be glo - ry and praise!

Copyright © 1976 by Medical Mission Sisters, Phil., Pa.

Liberation

First Voice

Deliver us from bondage, Lord,
from the threat of a thousand chariots
barreling down our backs.
Deliver us from doing to others
what we detest done to ourselves.
Deliver us from that hypocrisy
that waits till the sea has parted
and the din of fear falls deathly still
to in turn become pursuer,
dispensing oppressive burdens
we would not, could not, bear.
Deliver us from evil, Lord,
from the role of the oppressor
and the lot of the oppressed.
Deliver us from ourselves.

Second Voice

The devastating wind of winter
falls flush upon our plans
and whines.
All in a rush
my soul
knows just how much its narrowness
confines.

Scripture

Hear, you deaf;
   and look, you blind, that you may see!
Who is blind but my servant,
   or deaf as my messenger whom I send?
Who is blind as my dedicated one,
   or blind as the servant of the Lord?
[Who] sees many things, but does not observe them;
   [whose] ears are open, but . . . does not hear.
This is a people robbed and plundered,
   they are all of them trapped in holes and hidden in prisons;
they have become a prey with none to rescue,
   a spoil with none to say, "Restore!"
Who among you will give ear to this,
   will attend and listen for the time to come? (Isa. 42:18-20, 22, 23)

62

Litany for Personal Liberation
          Respond to each invocation with: DELIVER US, LORD!

Leader: From a lack of concern . . .   *All:* Deliver us, Lord!
                 From a love of ease . . .
                 From a need for power . . .
                 From too narrow a view . . .
                 From disillusionment . . .
                 From selfishness and greed . . .
                 From a tendency to manipulate . . .
                 From too little love . . .
                 From intolerance to change . . .
                 From insensitivity to others . . .
                 From attitudes that are superficial and insincere . . .
                 From every kind of bondage . . .

Scripture   For freedom Christ has set us free; stand fast
                 therefore, and do not submit again to a yoke of
                 slavery. For you were called to freedom . . . only
                 do not use your freedom as an opportunity for the
                 flesh, but through love be servants of one another.
                                                        (Gal. 5:1, 13)

Prayer   We turn to you, liberating Spirit.
                 Sensitive to our insufficiencies,
                 we long to be freed from bondage
                 to enjoy the glorious liberty
                 that belongs to the children of God.
                 Break these chains
                 we endure for the sake of the gospel,
                 that all may know
                 beyond a doubt
                 there is no chaining the Word of God
                 made flesh in Christ Jesus,
                 Liberator and Lord. Amen.

Pause for Silent Prayer

Third Voice   The song of the street is silent.
                 Dreamer, hang up your harp!
                 Nation has set upon nation
                 laying waste to wisdom,
                 subjecting color and by all means creed
                 to the scourge of captivity.
                 Who will break bread for the hungry?
                 Justice is but a bouncing ball
                 in a politicians' game.
                 "Where is your God?" the puppets tease.
                 Yet all the weary while long
                 the watchful wait

63

and still believe
mourning will turn into dancing
and sadness into song.

Scripture   Thus says God, Yahweh, . . . who created
the heavens and spread them out,
who gave shape to the earth and what comes from it,
who gave breath to its people
and life to the creatures that move in it:
I, Yahweh, have called you to serve the cause of right;
I have taken you by the hand and formed you;
I have appointed you as a covenant of the people
   and light of the nations,
to open the eyes of the blind,
to free captives from prison,
and those who live in darkness from the dungeon.
                                              (Isa. 42:5-7 JB)

Action   *The challenge facing Christians today is to make God's Word specific, to match gospel mandates to our needs now. Take a bowl containing small slips of paper—prepared before the service began—each slip naming a contemporary ill in need of liberation: HUNGER, POVERTY, VIOLENCE, EXPLOITATION, DISEASE, UNREST, and so forth. There should be at least as many papers as there are people present. Pass the bowl around, and invite each person to draw out a slip of paper. The word written there will be that individual's special area of concern and focal point for prayer.*

+ *Prayer of the Faithful*
    Let each person in turn read aloud what is written on his or her slip of paper. In this way, the community places society's needs before the Lord in prayer.
    To each need, let the whole group respond: DELIVER US, LORD!
    (i.e., From HUNGER . . . Deliver us, Lord!
        From OPPRESSION . . . etc.)

+ *Project for the Month*
    Invite each person to make that category of need the object of intense prayer during the coming month. Try to make that general category more specific by linking it to items in the news.

        Suggestion: Put your slip of paper with its particular society ill on your bulletin board or mirror or refrigerator door. Find a pertinent scripture passage and pin that beside it. Be attentive to news items, to clippings and photos in newspapers, magazines, and journals that make this need very specific. Be sure to make each "for instance" the object of your prayer. For example, if you should draw the word HUNGER, you might find yourself praying for victims of a famine in India or for a rainfall in the Sudan. Contrasting pictures or stories also stimulate awareness, such as photos of elegant cuisine next to a sketch of a starving child.

    The group might like to meet again the following month to share facts and feelings, perhaps to continue the project by drawing a different area of need. Besides its obvious prayer value, this approach builds awareness, a necessary first step in the struggle for social justice.

64

Leader: Happy is the one whose help is the God of Jacob,
whose hope is in the Lord . . .
who made heaven and earth,
the sea, and all that is in them;
who keeps faith for ever;
who executes justice for the oppressed;
who gives food to the hungry.
The Lord sets the prisoners free;
the Lord opens the eyes of the blind.
The Lord lifts up those who are bowed down. . . .
Praise the Lord!   (Ps. 146:5-8, 10)

All: The spirit of the Lord Yahweh has been given to me,
for Yahweh has anointed me,
   has sent me to bring good news to the poor,
to bind up hearts that are broken;
to proclaim liberty to captives,
freedom to those in prison;
to proclaim a year of favour. (Isa. 61:1-2 JB)

Prayer Lord, you search us and know us.
How mysterious are your ways.
You send those of us already captive
to free others from their chains,
those who are hurt, even broken,
to bind another's wounds.
Yet we know that the light
we bring to others
will be dawn to our own darkness,
for in giving, we receive,
in releasing from bondage
we experience liberation,
in rebuilding ruins
we are made whole
through Christ our Lord. Amen.

Song Try Pete Seeger's "One Man's Hands" (There is so little we can do alone, but
   when "two and two and fifty make a million," we hasten that day of the
   Lord.)
Or perhaps "Song of Liberation" or "Day of Justice," both from the album
Sandstone, by the Medical Mission Sisters.

Song of Liberation

Key: Cm CAPO: 3rd Play Am

Words and music by
Sister Miriam Therese Winter

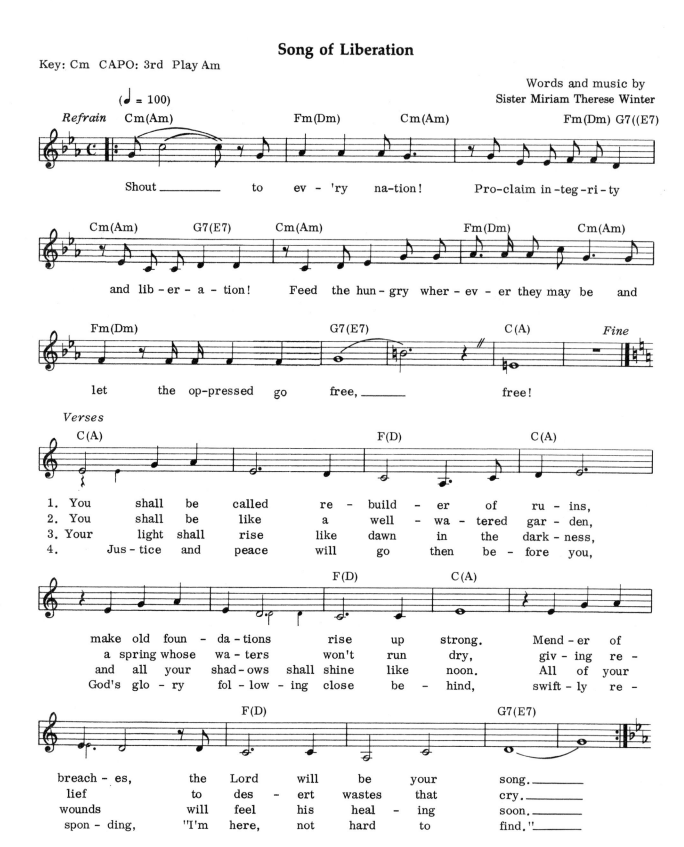

1. You shall be called re-build-er of ru-ins,
2. You shall be like a well-wa-tered gar-den,
3. Your light shall rise like dawn in the dark-ness,
4. Jus-tice and peace will go then be-fore you,

make old foun-da-tions rise up strong. Mend-er of
a spring whose wa-ters won't run dry, giv-ing re-
and all your shad-ows shall shine like noon. All of your
God's glo-ry fol-low-ing close be-hind, swift-ly re-

breach-es, the Lord will be your song._____
lief to des-ert wastes that cry._____
wounds will feel his heal-ing soon._____
spon-ding, "I'm here, not hard to find."_____

© MCMLXXVIII by Medical Mission Sisters, Phil., Pa. Reprinted by permission Vanguard Music Corp., 250 W. 57th St., N.Y., N.Y. 10019

Be Reconciled

Scripture   For anyone who is in Christ, there is a new creation; the old creation has gone, and now the new one is here. It is all God's work. It was God who reconciled us . . . through Christ and gave us the work of handing on this reconciliation. In other words, God in Christ was reconciling the world, . . . not holding [our] faults against [us], and . . . has entrusted to us the news that all are reconciled. So we are ambassadors for Christ; it is as though God were appealing through us, and the appeal that we make in Christ's name is: be reconciled to God. For our sake God made the sinless one into sin, so that in him we might become the goodness of God. As his fellow workers, we beg you once again not to neglect the grace of God that you have received. For he says: At the favorable time I have listened to you; on the day of salvation I came to your help. Well, now is the favorable time; this is the day of salvation. (II Cor. 5:17-21, 6:1-2 JB)

Gather in a circle, with chairs facing out. During the following prayer for forgiveness, reflect privately, together, on our individual and corporate need for reconciliation.

Prayer for Forgiveness
Each petition voiced by the leader should be followed by a brief period of silence, which will be terminated by the leader's LORD, HAVE MERCY! All then respond with the sung refrain: GRANT TO US, O LORD as indicated below.

Sung refrain (All)   Lucien Deiss

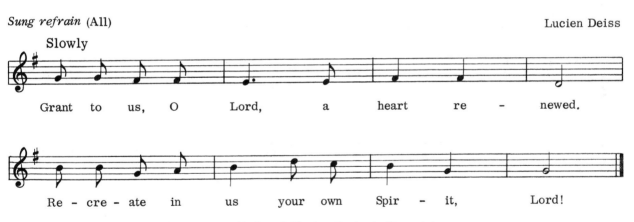

Grant to us, O Lord, a heart re - newed.

Re - cre - ate in us your own Spir - it, Lord!

© 1965 World Library Publications. Reprinted with permission.

Leader: We ask forgiveness for all those times we have closed
our hearts to the promptings of the Spirit and
narrowed our horizons to what has been comfortable
and safe.
                              Silence . . . Response
         Leader: LORD HAVE MERCY!   *All:* GRANT TO US . . .
We ask forgiveness for our failure to be risk-takers often.
                              Silence . . . Response
We ask forgiveness for the times we have been bitter,
for the times we manipulated others to achieve our
own ends.

Silence . . . Response

We ask forgiveness for the violence around us and within
   us and for all those occasions when we failed to make peace.

Silence . . . Response

We ask forgiveness for our smugness, which gives rise
   to revolutions.

Silence . . . Response

We ask forgiveness for all the injustice we perpetuate
   and for upholding values the gospel abhors.

Silence . . . Response

We ask forgiveness for all those times when your Word
   remained mute in us while the world awaited the
   uplift of its song.

Silence . . . Response

We ask forgiveness for our cluttered lives and for our
   fear of approaching you empty-handed.

Silence . . . Response

We ask forgiveness for our lack of warmth that inhibits
   a welcoming spirit.

Silence . . . Response

We ask forgiveness for failing to be fully alive to
   our potential,
   for refusing to be people poured out for the sake of the gospel.

Silence . . . Response

First Reader	"But now, now—it is Yahweh who speaks— come back to me with all your heart, fasting, weeping, mourning." Let your hearts be broken, not your garments torn, turn to Yahweh your God again, who is all tenderness and compassion, slow to anger, rich in graciousness, and ready to relent. (Joel 2:12-13 JB)
Second Reader	"Lord, how often must I forgive my brother [or sister] if he [or she] wrongs me? As often as seven times?" (Matt. 18:21)
First Reader	Jesus answered, "Not seven, I tell you, but seventy-seven times" (Matt. 18:22 JB). "Yes, if you forgive others their failings, your heavenly Father will forgive you yours; but if you do not forgive others, your Father will not forgive your failings either . . . So you should pray like this:"
All	*Join hands, still facing outward, and pray the Lord's Prayer aloud .* *Move the chairs so that the circle now faces inward. Or stand up, walk around the chairs, and form an inner circle with everyone facing in.*
Blessing	May the God who is our Father fill that which is empty in us, complete that which is incomplete, mold with care that which is poorly formed, bring to life that which is dead; and through our Lord Jesus, all which causes emptiness or misdirection in our lives is forgiven, in the name of the Father, and of the Son, and of the Holy Spirit. Amen.

Song   "Be Reconciled" by Miriam Therese Winter (from the album *Sandstone*).

Gift

Gifts are meant for giving,
so give yourself away.
Many people are lifelong secrets,
enamored with the wrappings,
hesitant to peek inside:
it might not measure up!
All their lives
they must be content
to be less than they really are.
Why are we afraid to name our gift
except perhaps in private
and only now and then?
Embarrassment, indifference,
disdain, or disappointment
buries some talents soundly
like treasure hidden in a field
good news whispered cautiously
instead of whooped aloud.
Why can't we accept
and see
that everyone is gifted,
gift, even you
and me.

Discerning our gift

Setting the Mood

Song   "God Gives His People Strength" (from the album *Joy Is Like the Rain*)

Scripture   Now there are varieties of gifts, but the same Spirit; and there are varieties of service, but the same Lord; and there are varieties of working, but it is the same God who inspires them all in every one. To each is given the manifestation of the Spirit for the common good. To one is given through the Spirit the utterance of wisdom, and to another the utterance of knowledge according to the same Spirit, to another faith by the same Spirit, to another gifts of healing by the one Spirit, to another the working of miracles, to another prophecy, to another the ability to distinguish between spirits, to another various kinds of tongues, to another the interpretation of tongues. All these are inspired by one and the same Spirit, who apportions to each one individually as [God] wills.

(I Cor. 12:4-11)

Prayer Come, O creative Spirit,
enlighten us that we might discern
the unique and precious gift
that is the person that we are.
You distribute your splendor wisely
for the sake of the common good.
Let us see, share, and celebrate
your wonderful work in us,
through Jesus Christ, Gift of the Father,
forever and ever. Amen

Silent Reflection

Reflect quietly on the following questions (approximately ten minutes). Try to answer honestly:

1   *What quality in yourself do you most value? What makes you especially happy to say, "That's me!"*

2   *What do you feel is your gift to this particular group (family, community, church)?*

Sharing our gift

Form into groups of four to provide an opportunity for listening and sharing. In turn, one at a time, let each person entrust to the group his or her response to the questions above. Affirmative listening is preferred to dialogue or discussion. When all the groups have finished, reassemble into one large gathering.

Celebrating our gift

Reading A revolution is going on in the world today that is cutting across lines of class, color, and nationality. It is the revolution of those all over the world who are in on the secret of gifts. At the heart of it is the gospel, but the church cannot assert this in the traditional words of the faith because of a noisy piety that failed to become embodied in authentic life styles. In this revolution, one gift is neither superior nor inferior to another. The recognition dawns that the exercising of gifts is wrapped up with our needs which mesh with corresponding needs in the world . . . Because our gifts carry us out into the world and make us participants in life, the uncovering of them is one of the most important tasks confronting any one of us. When we talk about being true to ourselves—being the persons we are intended to be—we are talking about gifts . . . We ask to know the will of God without guessing that this will is written into our very beings. We perceive that will when we discern our gifts. Our obedience and surrender to God are in large part our obedience and surrender to our gifts.

(Elizabeth O'Connor, *Eighth Day of Creation*)

Summary Prayer Good and generous Father,
you gave us eternal life
when you gifted us with your Son.
He in turn gave his life for us
that we might be cheerful givers,
aware that the greatest gift of all
is to lay down our lives in love.
Teach us to be more sensitive
to the gift of one another,
convinced that what each person offers

is precisely what we need.
We promise to let our light shine
across this dark and troubled world,
to glorify you and praise you,
Giver of gifts. Amen.

Benediction Grace was given to each of us
according to the measure of Christ's gift (Eph. 4:7). Amen!
Having gifts that differ
according to the grace given to us,
let us use them (Rom. 12:6). Amen!
Give, and it will be given to you;
for the measure you give
will be the measure you get back (Luke 6:38). Amen!
You have heard the Word of the Lord!
Go forth now
and live generously.
Be at peace with your gift
and grateful
to the Father, the Son, and the Holy Spirit.
Amen!

Song "Simple Gifts" (traditional Shaker hymn) or "God Loves A
Cheerful Giver" or "What Do You Ask of Me?" (from the albums *I
Know the Secret* and *Remember Me*, by the Medical Mission Sisters)

Name

This might be the basis for a commitment service, such as dedication to a task or ministry, or simply a prayer to reorder priorities. Several items are needed: name tags with a peel-away piece on the back for easy adherence to a garment, or the equivalent; pens or pencils for writing one's name; a large piece of felt (two yards or more, depending on the size of the group) or similar cloth to serve as a banner background. Before the prayer begins, take a piece of chalk and outline a big circle on the cloth, then hang it in a prominent place, or in an informal setting, place it on a nearby table.

Part One—I HAVE CALLED YOU BY YOUR NAME, YOU ARE MINE!

To name means more than to label.
To name is to bring into focus,
bestow a bit of meaning,
believe that one is or can become
the reality so named.
To be named is to be known
enough
to be called upon
or claimed.
To name is to call into being
or invite into relationship
and hope for a response.
Here I am! implies commitment.
When we tell our names
or register,
we hand over our very persons.
Numbers can never mean enough.
Much depends on names.

In order to experience the significance of naming in Scripture, time will be spent getting in touch with God's Word and integrating, through sung response and silences, what it seems to say to us.

Sung response to Scripture selections (All)

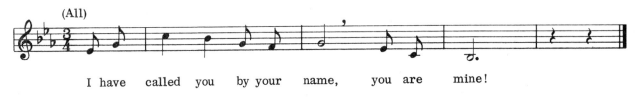

I have called you by your name, you are mine!

Copyright © 1978 by Medical Mission Sisters, Phil., Pa.

Scripture   Out of the ground the Lord God formed every beast of the field and every bird of the air, and brought them to the man to see what he would call them; and whatever the man called every living creature, that was its name . . . The man called his wife's name Eve, because she was the mother of all living. (Gen. 2:19; 3:20)

> *All:* I have called you . . .

Do not be afraid, for I have redeemed you;
I have called you by your name, you are mine.
Should you pass through the sea, I will be with you;
or through rivers, they will not swallow you up.
Should you walk through fire, you will not be scorched
and the flames will not burn you.
For I am Yahweh, your God,
the Holy One of Israel, your saviour. (Isa. 43:1-3 JB)

> *All:* I have called you . . .

I will make you a great nation; I will bless you and make your name so famous that it will be used as a blessing . . . As the new heavens and the new earth I shall make will endure before me . . . so will your race and name endure. (Gen 12:2; Isa. 66:22 JB)

> *All:* I have called you . . .

The nations then will see your integrity,
all the kings your glory,
and you will be called by a new name,
one which the mouth of Yahweh will confer.
You are to be a crown of splendour in the hand of Yahweh,
a princely diadem in the hand of your God;
no longer are you to be named "Forsaken",
nor your land "Abandoned",
but you shall be called "My Delight"
and your land "The Wedded";
for Yahweh takes delight in you
and your land will have its wedding. (Isa. 62:2-4 JB)

> *All:* I have called you . . .

The seventy returned with joy, saying, "Lord, even the demons are subject to us in your name!" And he said to them . . . "Do not rejoice in this, that the spirits are subject to you; but rejoice that your names are written in heaven." (Luke 10:17-20)

> *All:* I have called you . . .

Hear what the Spirit says to the churches. To the one who conquers I will give some of the hidden manna, and I will give a white stone, with a new name written on the stone which no one knows except [the one] who receives it. (Rev. 2:17)

> *All:* I have called you . . .

Lo, on Mount Zion stood the Lamb, and with him a hundred and forty-four thousand who had his name and his Father's name written on their foreheads. (Rev. 14:1)

> *All:* I have called you . . .

Silent Reflection

Action Distribute name tags to all present. Ask each person to write his or her name on the tag—first name, full name, nickname, whatever—as each prefers to be called. Put the name tag on and wear it during the rest of the service.

Part Two—OUR FATHER, WHO ART IN HEAVEN, HALLOWED BE THY NAME!

"God is bountiful to men, but most of them give no thanks" (Koran: Surah 10:60; 27:73). Here in its double sense is the situation between God and us, the initiative of grace and the response of recognition. In this relation is the whole of religion. For Islam it hinges upon the Beautiful Names by which God is at once denoted in his goodness and acknowledged in gratefulness and dependence. In his names he is described and by his names he is invoked. They are then the crossing points in a divine manwardness and a human Godwardness. They are at once clues of theology and the stuff of prayer. "God's are the beautiful Names, so call upon him by them" (Surah 7:180). Plainly, there is no invoking God, which is not also a describing of him. The primary purpose of what we may call God's nameability is that he may be invoked. Names, human or divine, would not be necessary unless there were intercourse. They are the vocabulary of converse and relationship. Both biblically and quaranically, we find that God's names are the ground of his accessibility. Calling him, for example, "O thou Provider," and calling upon him to provide, are synonymous. They mean precisely the same thing. The mention of the name is in itself the plea. So it is that much of Muslim prayer, outside the ritual worship, is the simple ejaculation of his names, with no further petition. In simply naming God, one is calling upon him "in that name," and awaiting his answer to the description. The utterance of the name is plea as well as worship. In effect the suppliant is saying: "Be, O God, what thou art." In calling upon God we must know whereby he is called. Our pleas rest upon his character, as such character, delineated in his names, comes within our knowledge. He has given us names to invoke him because he is in vital relation to our lives. God's having names, usable of him and to him, by us, means that our knowledge of him has living significance. He is not a formula with which to conclude a debate, not an abstraction to grace a theory. He has names!

(Kenneth Cragg, *The Dome and the Rock*)

Sung response to scripture selections (All)

Our   Fa - ther, who   art   in   heav - en,   hal-lowed   be   thy   name!

Copyright © 1978 by Medical Mission Sisters, Phil., Pa.

Scripture Then Moses said to God, "If I come to the people of Israel and say to them, 'The God of your fathers has sent me to you,' and they ask me, 'What is his name?' what shall I say to them?" God said to Moses, "I AM WHO I AM." And [God] said, "Say this to the people of Israel, 'I AM has sent me to you.' " (Exod. 3:13, 14)

(All) Our Father, who art in heaven . . .

And the Lord said to Moses, "This very thing that you have spoken I will do; for you have found favor in my sight, and I know you by name." Moses said,

"I pray thee, show me thy glory." And [God] said, "I will make all my goodness pass before you, and will proclaim before you my name 'The Lord'; and I will be gracious to whom I will be gracious, and will show mercy on whom I will show mercy." (Exod. 33:17-19)
   (All)   Our Father, who art in heaven . . .

Behold, a virgin shall conceive and bear a son, and his name shall be called Emmanuel (which means, God with us). (Isa. 7:14, Matt. 1:23)
   (All)   Our Father, who art in heaven . . .

That which is conceived in her is of the Holy Spirit; she will bear a son, and you shall call his name Jesus, for he will save his people from their sins. (Matt. 1:20-21)
   (All)   Our Father, who art in heaven . . .

For to us a child is born,
   to us a son is given,
and the government will be upon his shoulder,
   and his name will be called
   "Wonderful Counselor, Mighty God,
   Everlasting Father, Prince of Peace." (Isa. 9:6)
   (All)   Our Father, who art in heaven . . .

Go therefore and make disciples of all nations, baptizing them in the name of the Father and of the Son and of the Holy Spirit. (Matt. 28:19)
   (All)   Our Father, who art in heaven . . .

To all who received him, who believed in his name, he gave power to become children of God. (John 1:12)
   (All)   Our Father, who art in heaven . . .

Where two or three are gathered in my name, there am I in the midst of them. (Matt. 18:20)
   (All)   Our Father, who art in heaven . . .

Whatever you ask in my name, I will do it, that the Father may be glorified in the Son. (John 14:13)
   (All)   Our Father, who art in heaven . . .

"Teacher, we saw a man casting out demons in your name, and we forbade him, because he was not following us." But Jesus said, "Do not forbid him; for no one who does a mighty work in my name will be able soon after to speak evil of me. For [whoever] is not against us is for us. For truly, I say to you, whoever gives you a cup of water to drink because you bring the name of Christ, will by no means lose [a] reward." (Mark 9:38-41)
   (All)   Our Father, who art in heaven . . .

There is salvation in no one else, for there is no other name under heaven given among [us] by which we must be saved. (Acts 4:12)
   (All)   Our Father, who art in heaven . . .

He humbled himself and became obedient unto death, even death on a cross. Therefore God has highly exalted him and bestowed on him the name which is above every name, that at the name of Jesus every knee should bow, in heaven and on earth and under the earth, and every tongue confess that Jesus is Lord, to the glory of God the Father. (Phil. 2:8-11)
   (All)   Our Father, who art in heaven . . .

Silent Reflection
Action   *Let spontaneous prayer rise out of the silence. Call on God by calling aloud those wonderful, revealing names—Peacemaker . . . All-Merciful . . . Redeemer—knowing that to invoke a name is in fact to ask for what that name implies: peace, mercy, redemption.*

Part Three—PRAISE THE NAME OF THE LORD!

Antiphonal Prayer of Praise
   Divide the community into two groups, group A and B. Pray the following verses aloud as a two-part choir.

   A: Praise, O servants of the Lord, praise the name of the Lord!
   B: Blessed be the name of the Lord, from this time forth
        and forevermore!
   A: From the rising of the sun to its setting
        the name of the Lord is to be praised! (Ps. 113:1-3)
   B: Our help is in the name of the Lord,
        who made heaven and earth. (Ps. 124:8)
   A: I will sing praise to the name of the Lord, the Most High. (Ps. 7:17*b*)
   B: Blessed is he who comes in the name of the Lord!
        Hosanna in the highest! (Matt. 21:9)
   A: Those who acknowledge your name can rely on you. (Ps. 9:10 JB)
   B: The Lord gave, and the Lord has taken away;
        blessed be the name of the Lord. (Job 1:21)
   A: Sing to God, sing praises to [God's] name;
   B: that name is the Lord, rejoice! (Ps. 68:4*)
   A: I will tell of your name to my brethren. (Ps. 22:22)
        I will cause your name to be celebrated in all generations. (Ps. 45:17)
   B: O magnify the Lord with me, and let us exalt
        [God's] name together! (Ps. 34:3)
   A: Yahweh, our Lord, how great your name throughout the earth! (Ps. 8:1 JB)
   B: All my life I will bless you
        in your name lift up my hands. (Ps. 63:4 JB)
   A: I face your holy temple,
        bow down and praise your name
      because of your constant love and faithfulness,
   B: because you have shown that your name
      and your commands are supreme. (Ps. 138:2)
   A: Bless the Lord, O my soul;
      and all that is within me,
        bless [God's] holy name! (Ps. 103:1)
   B: Blessed be that glorious name for ever;
        may [God's] glory fill the whole earth! (Ps. 72:19)

Benediction
   Leader   Our help is in the name of the Lord.
   All   Who made heaven and earth.

   Leader   Grace and peace be with us all
              in the name of the Father,
              and of the Son,
              and of the Holy Spirit.
   All   Amen.

Action   As a closing action, invite all present to recommit themselves to the Lord. To symbolize this renewed covenant, go forward as a group—spontaneously or in formal procession—or one by one, to place your name tag within the chalk circle outlined on the banner cloth. Name tags with adhesive backing will adhere easily without pins, glue, or stitching. To make the gesture more meaningful, remind the group that the surrendering of a name means the handing over of a person, without qualification. As you place your name, yourself, at God's disposal, pray silently that name by which God is special to you.

Song suggestions

During the final action, the group could sing Clarence Rivers' "Bless the Lord" ("Glory to God, glory . . O praise the name of the Lord!") . . . or Stephen Somerville's setting of Psalm 8: "Yahweh, our Lord, how wonderful your name throughout the earth!" . . . or Miriam Therese Winter's song "Wonderful!" from the collection Gold, Incense and Myrrh.

Note: *At the close of the service, transform the circle filled with names into a flower by adding brightly colored, oval-shaped pieces of cloth or paper around its rim. Faith flowers more fully through corporate commitment, when we reveal and surrender ourselves to one another and to God. Add leaves, a stem, and other touches, even a text, if you wish. During Eastertide, that circle could become a sun by adding yellow triangles instead of ovals. Other symbols might be appropriate to the season: the outline of a cross to which we add our own names during Lent; or the word YES that remains empty until we flesh out the letters with ourselves. After the service, when the full banner is complete, display it in your church or community. You might prefer to have the banner already decorated before the service, so that the names to be added provide that final, finishing touch.*

Clay Pots

All: Yahweh, you are our Father;
we the clay, you the potter;
we are all the work of your hand.(Isa. 64:8 JB)

Reader: The word that came to Jeremiah from the Lord: "Arise, and go
down to the potter's house, and there I will let you hear my
words." So I went down to the potter's house, and there he was
working at his wheel. And the vessel he was making of clay was
spoiled in the potter's hand, and he reworked it into another
vessel, as it seemed good to the potter to do. (Jer. 18:1-4)

All: Yahweh, you are our Father;
we the clay, you the potter;
we are all the work of your hand.

Reader: Then the word of the Lord came to me: "O house of Israel, can I not do with you
as this potter has done? says the Lord. Behold, like the clay in the potter's hand,
so are you in my hand." (Jer. 18:5,6)

All: Yahweh, you are our Father;
we the clay, you the potter;
we are all the work of your hand.

Reader: Shall the potter be regarded as the clay;
that the thing should say of its maker,
    "He did not make me";
or the thing formed say of
[the one] who formed it,
    "He has no understanding"?
                    (Isa. 29:16)

All: Yahweh, you are our Father;
we the clay, you the potter;
we are all the work of your hand.

Reader: Woe to you who strive with your Maker,
an earthen vessel with the potter!
Does the clay say to whoever fashions it,
'What are you making?' or
'Your work has no handles.'? (Isa. 45:9-10)

All: Yahweh, you are our Father;
we the clay, you the potter;
we are all the work of your hand.

Reader: Has the potter no right over the clay, to make out of the same lump one vessel for beauty and another for menial use? What if God, desiring to show . . . wrath and to make known . . . power, has endured with much patience vessels of wrath made for destruction, in order to make known the vessels of mercy, which [have been] prepared beforehand for glory. (Rom. 9:21-23)

> *All:* Yahweh, you are our Father;
> we the clay, you the potter;
> we are all the work of your hand.

Song   "Spirit of God" (verse one)

> Spirit of God in the clear running water,
> blowing to greatness the trees on the hill.
> Spirit of God in the finger of morning,
> fill the earth, bring it to birth
> and blow where you will.
>> Blow, blow, blow till I be
>> but breath of the Spirit blowing in me.

© MCMLXV by Medical Mission Sisters, Phil., Pa. Reprinted by permission Vanguard Music Corp., 250 W. 57th St., N.Y., N.Y. 10019

Reflection   You have made me endless, such is your pleasure.
This frail vessel you empty again and again,
and fill it ever with fresh life.
This little flute of a reed
you have carried over hills and dales,
you have breathed through it melodies eternally new.
At the immortal touch of your hands
my little heart loses its limits in joy
and gives birth to utterance ineffable.
Your infinite gifts come to me
only on these very small hands of mine.
Ages pass, and still you pour,
and still there is room to fill.
          (Rabindranath Tagore, *Gitanjali*)

Response   (Solo voice)

> Strange:
> water to wine
> yet we do not change,
> wine into blood
> and blood
> food
> yet we are unchanged
> though often renewed.
> We are dry vessels:
> fill us up!
> But Lord
> do not jar
> my little cup.

Silent Prayer
Response *(All)*   God . . . has given us this work to do, and so we do not become discouraged. . . . Yet we who have this spiritual treasure are like common clay pots, in order to show that the supreme power belongs to God, not to us. We are often troubled, but not crushed; sometimes

in doubt, but never in despair; there are many enemies, but we are never without a friend; and though badly hurt at times, we are not destroyed. At all times we carry in our mortal bodies the death of Jesus, so that his life also may be seen in our bodies. Throughout our lives we are always in danger of death for Jesus' sake, in order that his life may be seen in this mortal body of ours. This means that death is at work in us, but life is at work in you. (II Cor. 4:1, 7-12, TEV)

Prayer   *(Leader)*   Lord God of power and might,
you made us fragile and tentative,
that you alone might be our strength,
vulnerable, easily hurt,
to entice us to tenderness.
Help us to understand
that we who would minister to a broken world
must give to the point of breaking,
for to risk the cross is to guarantee
that we will be remolded
through the merits of redeeming love.
We come before you empty.
Empower us with your Spirit,
brimful and overflowing,
to nourish the ends of the earth. Amen.

Song   "Spirit of God" (verse three)
Spirit of God, everyone's heart is lonely,
watching and waiting and hungry until . . .
Spirit of God, we long that you only
fulfill the earth, bring it to birth
and blow where you will.
    Blow, blow, blow till I be
    but breath of the Spirit blowing in me.

Promises

Our lives are made up of promises,
pledges bonding individuals or groups
together for mutual good. A promise
implies surrender, and that means risk.
Will it be worth the effort? Is there
hope of continuity or is this a passing
thing? How can I cast an unqualified
yes into the unknown? Promises have
to prove themselves, and that takes time.
We waited from Creation to Christmas
for God's promise to come true. All
we can guarantee is the first step,
that leap into uncertainty, and wait,
try, trust. A promise calls out the
best in us by holding us to our word.
God, who is full of promises, insists
that those of us courageous enough to
make a promise can be constant enough
to keep it.

Scripture Reflection

Leader: Here is the sign of the Covenant I make between myself and you and every living creature with you for all generations. I set my bow in the clouds and it shall be a sign of the Covenant between me and the earth.   (Gen. 9:12-13 JB)

All: Keep your promise to me, your servant, the promise you made to those who obey you.   (Ps. 119:38)

Leader: Do not be afraid; you have won God's favor. The Holy Spirit will come upon you . . . and the power of the Most High will cover you with its shadow. And so the child will be holy and will be called Son of God.   (Luke 1:30, 35-36 JB)

All: Blessed is she who believed that the promise made her by the Lord would be fulfilled.   (Luke 1:45 JB)

Leader: Of one thing I am certain: the One who started the good work in you will bring it to completion by the Day of Christ Jesus.   (Phil. 1:6)

All: Blessed be the Lord . . . not one word has failed of all those generous promises.   (I Kings 8:56 based on RSV*)

Leader: My grace is sufficient for you, for my power is made perfect in weakness. (II Cor. 12:9)

All: Remember the word you pledged your servant,
on which you have built my hope.
This has been my comfort . . .
that your promise gives me life. (Ps. 119:49-50 JB)

Leader: There is no limit to the blessings which God can send you—[God] will make sure that you always have all you need for yourselves in every possible circumstance, and still have something to spare for all sorts of good works. (II Cor. 9:8 JB)

All: Show me how much you love me, Lord, and save me according to your promise. (Ps. 119:41 TEV)

Silent Reflection

Scripture Our great desire is that each one of you keep up [your] eagerness to the end, so that the things you hope for will come true. We do not want you to become lazy, but to be like those who believe and are patient, and so receive what God has promised. (Heb. 6:11-12 TEV)

The Promise *Those concerned are now invited to make their promise or vow before the Lord and in the presence of the community . . . or to renew promises already made if this occasion is an anniversary or jubilee.*

Affirmation of the Promise *(By the community)*

Leader: The Son of God, Jesus Christ, whom we preached among you . . . was not Yes and No; but in him it is always Yes. For all the promises of God find their Yes in him. That is why we utter the Amen through him, to the glory of God. (II Cor. 1:19-20)

All: *Sing the following response.*

Yes

© MCMLXX, MCMLXXI by Medical Mission Sisters, Phil., Pa. Reprinted by permission Vanguard Music Corp., 250 W. 57th St., N.Y., N.Y. 10019

Reading   Fidelity is an act of communion. It is not something one does but something one is. Fidelity is not measured by years but by the sheer intensity of a moment when a person breaks through to a new level of existence, a fresh state of being. Fidelity is not measured by permanence but by the utter transformation of the heart. The fidelity of last year may not be the fidelity of this year. Life, life is what you must affirm, no matter how painfully, even unwillingly. Life, at all costs, a life unfettered by the burden of selfishness, set free from the forms and norms which give the comfort but require the chains of enslavement. You are reliable only when others ascertain they will always find life in your presence. Others must know you as faithful, faithful so often that when they wonder where life lives, they will think of you as one of those in whom life has made a home.

(Anthony Padovano, *Free To Be Faithful*)

Prayer   God, our loving Father,
faithful through all generations
to your promises of grace,
we are confident that you will complete
this first step begun in us.
We commit ourselves wholeheartedly
to live worthy of our calling.
Send your Spirit as guarantee
that we will be always faithful,
proclaiming our YES not just today
but every day of our lives. Amen.

Song   Repeat "Yes to Celebration" several times.

Roots

Our roots are where we come from,
that tenacious hold on history
that is source of nourishment.
In the ruthless flux called "making it,"
we ache to connect with permanence
to counterbalance a shallow society's
stranglehold on us.
It is crucial that we be rooted
in someone, if not somewhere.
Pilgrim people on the move
root in relationships.
I am the vine, said Jesus,
extending himself through time and space
to graft us as branch.
To claim that continuity
we must submit to pruning,
sinking ourselves unconditionally
into the will of him in whom
we live and move and are.

Call to Prayer Since you have accepted Christ Jesus as Lord, live in union with him. Keep your roots deep in him, build your lives on him, and become stronger in your faith, as you were taught. And be filled with thanksgiving. (Col. 2:6-7 TEV)

Reflection I would not ask "who am I?"
if I knew; I would not talk
of roots if they were planted.
There are roots beyond our rootlessness
that even now reach through the sand
to soil, bedrock, and another world
that is born here . . .
The oneness of all elements
in the universe, which includes us,
has a root we know not of,
one common source of being
awake all night in earth's cellar,
refusing the final fall of any tree,

84

forcing it into new soil of life,
forcing us, earth, you and me,
to be roots to each other.   (James Carroll, *Elements of Hope*)

Silent Prayer

Reflection   Root of Jesse
rising
from many an ancient prophecy

promised child
to all who would be reconciled
breaks through at last.

A virgin shoot accepts
God's seed
bows to the Mighty Deed.
One branch
bears bud, flower, fruit:
Christ blossoms as David's root.

Lord, you are stem, stalk, tree!
Let your fruit take root in me.

Benediction I ask God from the wealth of . . . glory
to give you power through [the] Spirit
to be strong in your inner selves,
and I pray that Christ
will make his home in your hearts through faith.
I pray that you may have your roots
and foundation in love,
so that you, together with all God's people,
may have the power to understand
how broad and long,
how high and deep,
is Christ's love.
To [the One whose power working in us]
is able to do so much more
than we can ever ask for,
or even think of:
to God be the glory
in the church and in Christ Jesus
for all time,
forever and ever! Amen.
     (Eph. 3:16-18; 20-21 TEV; format changed by author)

Listening

How can we practice what we have not heard?
How will we hear when we do not listen?
How can we listen when we are seldom still?
The whole of the Christian message comes
down to sitting still. Everyone wants a
little listening, a personal presence that
peels away particulars, plunges beneath
the surface to encounter the core of reality
where healing happens. To listen like this
means prefering parables and fairy tales
and the cryptic approach of poetry to obvious,
more useful, facts. Insight is saved for
those who are certain that there is a deeper
meaning to even absurdity, that this is not
all there is. Be attentive then to your own
heart's demands hidden beneath your defenses.
Listen to the stories of others; and, when
surrounded by sounds or silences, stop often
to listen to God.

Scripture and Response
  Reader Listen to the Word of the Lord:

Then the disciples came to Jesus and asked him, "Why do you use parables when you talk to the people?" Jesus answered, "The knowledge about the secrets of the Kingdom of heaven has been given to you, but not to them. For the person who has something will be given more, so that he [or she] will have more than enough; but the person who has nothing will have taken away from him [or her] even the little he [or she] has. The reason I use parables in talking to them is that they look, but do not see, and they listen, but do not hear or understand. So the prophecy of Isaiah applies to them:

This people will listen and listen,
   but not understand;
they will look and look, but not see,
because their minds are dull,
   and they have stopped up their ears
   and have closed their eyes.

86

Otherwise, their eyes would see,
  their ears would hear,
  their minds would understand,
and they would turn to me, says God,
  and I would heal them.

"As for you, how fortunate you are! Your eyes see and your ears hear. I assure you that many prophets and many of God's people wanted very much to see what you see, but they could not, and to hear what you hear, but they did not.

"Listen, then, and learn what the parable of the sower means. Those who hear the message about the Kingdom but do not understand it are like the seeds that fell upon the path. The Evil One comes and snatches away what was sown in them. The seeds that fell on rocky ground stand for those who receive the message gladly as soon as they hear it. But it does not sink deep into them, and they don't last long. So when trouble or persecution comes because of the message, they give up at once. The seeds that fell among thorn bushes stand for those who hear the message; but the worries about this life and the love for riches choke the message, and they don't bear fruit. And the seeds sown in the good soil stand for those who hear the message and understand it: they bear fruit." (Matt. 13:10-23 TEV)

Refrain (All)   Speak; your servant is listening! (I Sam. 3:10 TEV)
(Leader)   And now, my [children], listen to me: happy are those
  who keep my ways. (Prov. 8:32)
        Refrain
Happy is the [person] who listens to me, watching
  daily at my gates, waiting beside my doors. (Prov. 8:34)
        Refrain
A bright cloud overshadowed them, and a voice from
  the cloud said, "This is my beloved Son, with whom
  I am well pleased; listen to him." (Matt. 17:5)
        Refrain
Listen to me, my people, and give ear to me, my nation;
  for a law will go forth from me, and my justice for
  a light to the peoples. (Isa. 51:4)
        Refrain
The Lord God will raise up for you a
  prophet from your [midst] as he raised me up.
  You shall listen to him in whatever he tells you.
  And it shall be that every soul that does not listen
  to that prophet shall be destroyed from the people. (Acts 3:22-23)
        Refrain
Be still, and know that I am God. (Ps. 46:10)
        Refrain

(Reader)   Listen once again to the Word of the Lord:

As Jesus and his disciples went on their way, he came to a village where a woman named Martha welcomed him in her home. She had a sister named Mary, who sat down at the feet of the Lord and listened to his teaching. Martha was upset over all the work she had to do, so she came and said, "Lord, don't you care that my sister has left me to do all the work by myself? Tell her to come and help me!" The Lord answered her, "Martha, Martha! You are worried and troubled over so many things, but just one is needed. Mary has chosen the right thing, and it will not be taken away from her." (Luke 10:38-42 TEV)

Silence   *Sit still for at least five minutes. God speaks to the listening heart.*

Reading   "We know more than we can tell, and we can tell nothing without relying on our awareness of things we may not be able to tell" somehow respond and correspond to the words "We are alone, you and I, and we cannot make one another unalone." We are alone, it seems, because we can know more than we can tell. If we could tell everything, we could become unalone. Because we are alone, because we cannot make one another unalone, there is "a time to embrace and a time to refrain from embracing" (Ecc. 3:5). Because we can know more than we can tell, because we cannot tell everything, there is "a time to keep silence and a time to speak" (Ecc. 3:7). Still, we can listen to one another, not only to the things we can tell but also to each other's awareness of things we may not be able to tell. Listening to the tacit element in what we are saying to one another, giving heed to the awareness of things we may not be able to tell, is like listening to the earth. It amounts to giving heed to the human situation out of which we are speaking, giving heed to the world of flesh in which we are dwelling as we speak of the spirit, giving heed to the world of spirit as we speak of the flesh . . . However divided a person is, if one listens not only to what he [or she] is saying but also to what he is relying on as he says it, one hears the whole human being. The listening itself, the giving of heed, is a giving of wholeness.

(John S. Dunne, *Time and Myth*)

Action   *Share an experience of listening, of giving heed in the sense of giving wholeness.*

Rearrange the group arbitrarily into pairs. If the number is uneven, form one group of three. The listening will occur within these sets.
Share with each other:
+ *a favorite scripture passage or verse*
Tell + *why it is special*
+ *what it says to you when you hear it*
+ *what message you listen for between the lines*
You may have to sit for awhile in silence before speaking in order to collect your thoughts. When one speaks, let the other really listen.
+ *After the sharing, regroup for the final benediction.*

Benediction

May the God whose Word is
   good news for us
open our hearts
   that we may listen and hear,
open our minds
   that we may appreciate and understand
how blessed are we
   who hear God's Word
   and do it
in the name of the Father,
   the Son,
   and the Spirit.
         Amen.

Song Paul Simon's "Sounds of Silence" (listen to the recording, or sing it) or Miriam Therese Winter's "Listen!"

Listen!

Key: E CAPO: 2nd Play D

Words and music by
Sister Miriam Therese Winter

Copyright © 1968 by Medical Mission Sisters, Phil., Pa.

Give Thanks

+ *The framework of this particular prayer is a Thanksgiving party. Giving thanks is appropriate anytime, but especially on Thanksgiving Day or on a day of special community significance, such as a jubilee or anniversary. If you should plan this party to coincide with our national Thanksgiving holiday, be sure to schedule it at a time that does not interfere with family traditions. The evening before, or even the Sunday before, seem best.*

+ *Well in advance of the occasion, announce to your community that plans are underway for a Thanksgiving party. You as a group need an opportunity to pause in the midst of very busy lives to acknowledge and be grateful for the reality that you are. Invite everyone to the party. Each person should plan to bring something that is the fruit of his or her labor, such as, a craft or hobby (needlework; a painting; a poem, song, or prayer; a homemade dress; a model airplane; a plant; a stamp collection; etc.) . . . or food for refreshments (cookies, cake, fudge, a favorite dessert) . . . whatever comes to mind when you ask yourself: "What skill or hobby do I especially enjoy—enough to share it with others and give thanks?"*

+ *Ask several people to take care of decorating and arranging the party room. Be sure to provide tables to accommodate what is brought.*

+ *Ask another group to prepare cold drinks or coffee, to receive the baked goods as they arrive and arrange them on a special table with the name of the donor beside each gift, and then serve refreshments at the appropriate time.*

+ *Gather several people to prepare a special slide show featuring the individuals and families of the community. The pictures should include highlights of the past year: projects, good works, special ministries (to shut-ins, the elderly, youth), community outreach, the liturgy, perhaps even some of the group's history, if this has been photographically chronicled. Ask someone with a facility for words to write a piece about the community—a personal reflection on its strengths and blessings—that can be illustrated with slides. Then ask each family to lend a favorite slide to be included in the program. Take some slides yourselves. Capture your church building, its ministerial staff, those who contribute supportive services, the surrounding neighborhood and any activities that reflect the tone of the community and its spirit. This slide show can have a mighty impact. People enjoy seeing themselves and their world projected on screen. It is also a public affirmation—a vote of thanks—for all the selfless and often silent services contributed by many throughout the year.*

The Event

It is good to give thanks to God.
It is good to give thanks to each other,
to take time out to be thankful
for the collective good that we are,
to take time out to realize
the grace of one and one.
Gratitude is the bedrock of society,
the solid, sure foundation
from which our goodness flows.
Appreciation, affirmation:
see it secure relationships.
See it change the world.

Antiphonal Setting of Psalm 136
To each verse proclaimed by the leader, all respond:
WHOSE LOVE IS EVERLASTING!

Leader: Give thanks to the Lord, who is good . . .   *All:*   Whose love is everlasting!
Give thanks to the God of Gods . . .
Give thanks to the Lord of lords . . .

Who performs wonderful deeds . . .
Whose wisdom made the heavens . . .
Who set the earth on the waters . . .

Who brought Israel out of Egypt . . .
with mighty hand and outstretched arm . . .
Who led the chosen people through the wilderness . . .

Who remembered us when we were down . . .
and snatched us from our oppressors . . .
Who provides for all living creatures . . .

Give thanks to the God of Heaven . . .

Scripture   May the peace of Christ reign in your hearts, because it is for this that you were called together as parts of one body. Always be thankful!
    Let the message of Christ, in all its richness, find a home with you. Teach each other, and advise each other, in all wisdom. With gratitude in your hearts sing psalms and hymns and inspired songs to God; and never say or do anything except in the name of the Lord Jesus, giving thanks to God the Father through him.   (Col. 3:15-17 JB)

Time of Sharing
+ *Hobby, craft, talent Show-and-Tell*
— *informally, if the group is large; a more direct and personal approach, if the group is small*
— *there may be some performance skill in the group; create a climate for talented individuals to sing, recite, play an instrument, or lead the group in song*
+ *Refreshments*
+ *Slide Show (as described above)*

Closing Prayer   We thank you, God our Father,
for your Spirit poured out upon us,
for the variety that enriches
the quality of our lives,

91

those up-front gifts that delight us all
and the steady, behind-the-scene-services
that enable us to carry on.
We thank you for all we have dared to do,
and especially for who we are.
Faith-filled and committed,
we pledge anew our energies
in the service of your people,
through Jesus Christ, our Savior and Lord,
forever and ever. Amen.

Song   "Thank You for Today" (The refrain appears at the beginning of the service. Sing the whole song, from the album *In Love*.)

Thank You

Song Refrain (All)

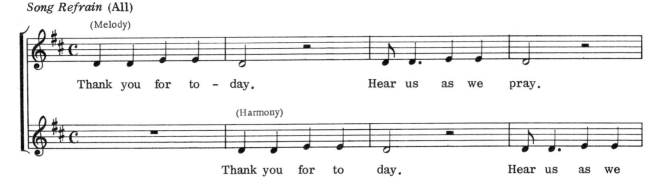

Thank you for to-day. Hear us as we pray.

Thank you for to day. Hear us as we

Give your Son to ev-'ry-one and stay _____ near.

pray. _____ Give your Son and stay _____ near.

© MCMLXVIII by Medical Mission Sisters, Phil., Pa. Reprinted by permission Vanguard Music Corp., 250 W. 57th St., N.Y., N.Y. 10019

Lovesong

A selection of pieces suitable for any celebration of love

> Love is patient and kind;
> love is not jealous or boastful;
> it is not arrogant or rude.
> Love does not insist on its own way;
> it is not irritable or resentful;
> it does not rejoice at wrong,
> but rejoices in the right.
> Love bears all things,
> believes all things,
> hopes all things,
> endures all things. (I Cor. 13:4-7)

Refrain *(All)* Let our love be genuine!

Reader Hate what is evil, hold fast to what is good.
> *Refrain*
Love one another with real affection.
> *Refrain*
Never lack zeal, be on fire with the Spirit, serve the Lord.
> *Refrain*
Rejoice in hope, be patient in tribulation, be constant in prayer.
> *Refrain*
Serve the community, practice hospitality.
> *Refrain*
Bless those who persecute you; bless and do not curse.
> *Refrain*
Rejoice with those who rejoice, weep with those who weep.
> *Refrain*
Live in harmony with one another.
> *Refrain*
Make real friends with the poor. Do not become self-satisfied.
> *Refrain*
Seek only the highest ideals. Do all you can to live at peace with everyone.
> *Refrain*
Do not be overcome by evil, but overcome evil with good.
> *Refrain*
> (Rom. 12:9-21 based on RSV*)

If you have real love you are inventive.
If you love, you try to find out, you are interested.
If you really love, you are patient, you are
    long-suffering.
Certainly if you love, you accommodate yourself.
If you love, you want to give, you are tireless,
    selfless and generous.
If you love, you really try to serve and not just work.
One does not spare oneself if one loves.

(Anna Dengel, foundress of the
Medical Mission Sisters)

Batter my heart, three personed God: for you
As yet but knock; breathe, shine, and seek to mend;
That I may rise and stand, o'erthrow me, and bend
Your force, to break, blow, burn, and make me new.
I, like an usurped town, to another due,
Labour to admit you, but oh, to no end;
Reason, your viceroy in me, me should defend,
But is captived, and proves weak or untrue.
Yet dearly I love you, and would be loved fain,
But am betrothed unto your enemy;
Divorce me, untie, or break that knot again,
Take me to you, imprison me, for I,
Except you enthrall me, never shall be free;
Nor ever chaste, except you ravish me.

(John Donne, "Batter My Heart")

Scripture Reflection
Divide the group into two choirs and recite the following scripture passages antiphonally.

One: You shall love Yahweh your God with all your heart, with all your soul, with all your strength. Let these words I urge on you today be written on your heart. (Deut. 6:5-6 JB)

Two: This is my commandment: . . . love one another as I have loved you. (John 15:12)

One: Anybody who receives my commandments and keeps them will be the one who loves me; and anybody who loves me will be loved by my Father. (John 14:21 JB)

Two: If you love me, you will keep my word, and my Father will love you, and we shall come to you and make our home with you. (John 14:23*)

One: I have loved you with an everlasting love; therefore I have continued my faithfulness to you. (Jer. 31:3)

Two: You can have no greater love than to lay down your life for your friends. (John 15:13*)

One: See how much the Father has loved us! His love is so great that we are called God's children—and so, in fact, we are. (I John 3:1 TEV)

Two: God showed his love for us by sending his only Son into the world, so that we might have life through him. This is what love is: it is not that we have loved God, but that he loved us and sent his Son. We love because God first loved us. (I John 4:9-10, 19 TEV)

One: Above everything, love one another earnestly, because love covers over many sins. (I Pet. 4:8 TEV)

Two:	Our love should not be just words and talk; it must be true love, which shows itself in action. (I John 3:18 TEV)
One:	I am certain that nothing can separate us from his love: neither death nor life, neither angels nor other heavenly rulers or powers, neither the present nor the future, neither the world above nor the world below—there is nothing in all creation that will ever be able to separate us from the love of God which is ours through Christ Jesus our Lord. (Rom. 8:38-39 TEV)
Two:	Love never ends. There are three things that last: faith, hope and love; and the greatest of these is love. (I Cor. 13:8, RSV, 13 JB)

Lovesong

A reflection on love's dynamic.
For anytime, but especially for
a time of leave-taking.

Love is patient, love is kind,
healing the hurt heart, haunting the mind.
Love will go with you, till one day you'll find,
love must leave love behind.

Love is a rainbow conceived in a storm.
Love, in the cold war of life, is warm.
Love will be waiting when evening draws on,
then one day, love may be gone.

Love is a mountain, certain and strong,
sometimes a silence, sometimes a song.
Love will remember the where and the when.
Come, love, come again.

Love will go tenderly, tenderly by,
teasing to laughter, teaching to cry.
Love will watch lovingly, letting you learn:
some loves never return.

Love will flow on into love without end.
Love will continue to break, to bend.
So soon December, remembering when.
Come, love, come again.

©MCMLXXVI by Medical Mission Sisters, Phil.,, Pa. Reprinted by permission Vanguard Music Corp; 250 W. 57th St., N.Y., N.Y.

Song of Songs

For a wedding, religious profession,
Eucharist, funeral, or any similar
surrender to love.

Here is the sign I give to you,
sign of the life I will live with you,
sign of our covenant, that you recall
Love linked to love linking one and all:

Come, come my beloved,
winter is over, the rains are done.

Come, welcome to laughter,
to love ever after, we run!
Love is a garden. Here is the key.
Eat of its honey. Taste love from me.
I am yours. You are mine.
Drink, drink deep of my wine.

Come, come my beloved.
Now the night beckons, fragrant with flowers.
Dream, dark is departing,
the day that is starting is ours!
Love is a fountain. Open its seal.
Dance in its waters. Let its touch heal
all the wounds you're weary of.
Take, take the gift of my love.

Come, come my beloved,
come from the desert into delight.
Wake, wake into wonder,
fear not the thunder or the night.
Love is a fire. Fierce is its flame.
Yield to its burning. Ask not its name.
While it warms, it consumes.
Love, love, come enter my rooms.

Come, come my beloved.
Winter is over, the rains are done.
Come, welcome to laughter.
To love ever after, we run, we run, we run!

© MCMLXXVIII by Medical Mission Sisters, Phil., Pa. Reprinted by permission Vanguard Music Corp., 250 W. 57th St., N.Y., N.Y. 10019

Returning

There is much to be said for harvests.
Why spend yourself sowing
just to throw it all away?
Reap the ripe, sweet succulence,
promise of warm memories
with winter coming on.
Wizened, weathered, mellower:
the heart would do well to be glad
that all its chores are done.
On that day, energies
that once billowed
like a kid's kite
in mid-March
will suddenly slacken,
respond
albeit reluctantly
to the soft tug
that brings love back
to its center and its source.
Summer's over.
Yes, I remember now.
And the sun will rise
in the ancient's eyes
to greet the child returning.
Merry Christmas . . .
Welcome home!

Summer Ends Now

Song "Try to Remember" by T. Jones-H. Schmidt
                    (from the show, The Fantastiks)

Reflection   Once we had our visions.
                Now we're content to dream our dreams,
                coping, as best we can,
                with every kind of loneliness,
                like absence, emptiness,
                and above all, letting go.
                The task now is remembering,
                savoring each past experience
                that crowds time's small horizon
                before the setting of our sun.
                We have reached the final threshold.
                The young call this fulfillment.
                We know it as old age
                pushing into retirement
                the best years of our lives.
                We are tired now.
                And restless.
                We must prepare to go.
                   "For all that has been, thanks!
                   To all that shall be, yes!"
                It was a glorious interim, Lord.
                Forgive us for looking back.

Scripture and Silences
        I have cared for you from the time you were born.
        I am your God and will take care of you
        until you are old and your hair is gray.
        I made you and will care for you;
        I will give you help and rescue you.
        "To whom will you compare me?" says the Lord.
        "Is there anyone else like me?" (Isa. 46:3-5 TEV)
                            Silence
        I tell you most solemnly,
        when you were young

98

you put on your own belt
and walked where you liked;
but when you grow old
you will stretch out your hands,
and somebody else will put a belt around you
and take you where you would rather not go.   (John 21:18 JB)
                        Silence
Bless Yahweh, my soul,
bless [God's] holy name, all that is in me!
Bless Yahweh, my soul,
and remember all the kindnesses:
in forgiving all your offenses,
in curing all your diseases,
in filling your years with prosperity,
in renewing your youth like an eagle's.   (Ps. 103:1-5 JB)
                        Silence
You alone are my hope, Lord, . . .
I have trusted you since my youth,
I have relied on you since I was born,
you have been my portion from my mother's womb,
and the constant theme of my praise.
Do not reject me now I am old,
nor desert me now my strength is failing.   (Ps. 71:5-6, 9 JB)
                        Silence
Aeons ago, you laid earth's foundations,
the heavens are the work of your hands;
all will vanish, though you remain,
all wear out like a garment,
like clothes that need changing you will change them;
but yourself, you never change, and your years are unending.   (Ps. 102:25-27 JB)
                        Silence
We never become discouraged. Even though our physical being is gradually
decaying, yet our spiritual being is renewed day after day. And this small and
temporary trouble we suffer will bring us a tremendous and eternal glory, much
greater than the trouble. For we fix our attention, not on things that are seen, but on
things that are unseen. What can be seen lasts only for a time, but what cannot be
seen lasts forever.   (II Cor. 4:16-18 TEV)

                        Silence

Reflection

He shall return
and we
as leaves dancing before the wind
shall feel the reeling
soul-revealing force of him
who soothes the sea
dares the dead to speak
delights in me.
Come, Lord Jesus!
It has been long enough.
Rouse this generation
from its deeply troubled sleep.

Keep your promise.
Do not delay,
but make haste to return again.
Amen.

A Film "The Stringbean"
Arrange to show this short but provocative film to the group. Follow it with small group discussions on insights gained from the experience. The film is available through your public library film service.

Discussion

Closing Song "Will You Be with Me?" by Miriam Therese Winter

Will You Be with Me?

Words and music by
Sister Miriam Therese Winter

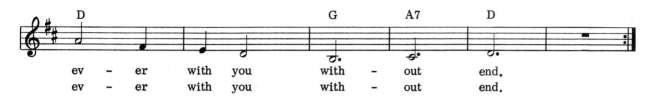

ev – er   with   you   with   –   out   end.

ev – er   with   you   with   –   out   end.

Copyright © 1971 by Medical Mission Sisters, Phil., Pa.

Letting Go

For a wake or a
funeral service
for any kind of gathering
in memory of the dead.

Reflection

We have mastered the moon and lengthened life but have yet to accomplish consistently the art of letting go. The bird in the hand, no matter how lean, is surety against not knowing. We prolong daylight indefinitely for fear of the ensuing dark, cling to summer hoping to delay the pain that lies ahead: routine desolation, irrevocable demands. Our death grip chokes what we value most. Some loves will not flower until we let them go.

Pause briefly for silent prayer

Let us speak now of dying, or as some say, passing on. Face it. A future is finished. All of a sudden a life we love is measured by its past. Grief overwhelms us. Yet we weep not for the one whose departure marks the goal of all our striving, but secretly for ourselves, for lost opportunities, and for all that might have been. The dead are in the hands of God but we, alive, are lonely. We cannot, will not, dare not, give in to that word "goodbye." Part of us died. We were not ready. We did not give consent. No rewards. No consolations. Ours is not fulfillment. We have simply been deprived. Yet if we really love this person more than we love ourselves, we will gladly let her (him) go: let go of our need of her (him), of that part of ourselves brought to life through her (him). Greater love than this we cannot have than to give up our life as we have known it, gladly, for our friend.

Pause briefly for silent prayer

Every starting over begins by letting go. To embrace the future we relinqish the past even as we love it, take leave of things as we would have them be . . . as they have always been . . . and welcome what they are. We claim a new mode of being only when we no longer owe allegiance to the old. What was is marked by absence and the penalty of loss. We embrace now a new kind of presence that will not go away again. Once before, for a little while, Love left to prepare a precedent, returning in Spirit full measure to abide till the end of time. Trust, if you can, this interim, the tenuous time between now and then, when we will know love beyond all imagining, beyond our own love's limited ability to satisfy. Cling then to love. It is constant. It is God alive in us. We were suckled since birth by the Lord of Life who will not leave us orphans or initiate an emptiness he does not intend to fill.

"The child cries out when from the
        right breast
the mother takes it away,
in the very next moment to find
        in the left one
its consolation."

Pause briefly for silent prayer

Song "God Gives His People Strength" (from the album *Joy Is Like the Rain* by the Medical Mission Sisters)

Remembering

Leader: *The leader invites the group into a time of sharing.*

Out of the silence, let the loved one, now deceased, take shape, become present, through shared memories, anecdotes, events—a story told simply, spontaneously, informally, without plan or preparation, by those who remember and rejoice.

Group: *Share reminiscences. No set time.*

Leader: *When the sharing has subsided, summarize the experience and prepare the group to move on.*

We have chronicled the personality of (_____) as we have known and loved her (him). The earthly phase of this precious life is closed, but the story continues, graced with a new beginning, a glorious continuity to climax what went before. May this sharing of memories be for us a transition to strength and courage. Having faced the past and our feelings of hurt, sorrow, loss, we prepare now to go forward in faith, with hope, through love, giving thanks for all that has been and praise for all that is now for (_____). Let us pray to God for the grace to accept all that will be for us.

Prayer (Leader) Let us pray:
God our loving Father,
your Son revealed that death leads to life.
We choose life, now and always,
no matter what the cost.
Give us the grace of letting go
and the courage to begin again,
through him, with him, and in him,
the Lord of Life. Amen.

Scripture and Response

Reading The souls of the virtuous are in the hands of God,
no torment shall ever touch them.
In the eyes of the unwise, they did appear to die,
their going looked like a disaster,
their leaving us, like annihilation;
but they are in peace.
If they experienced punishment as we see it,
their hope was rich with immortality;
slight was their affliction, great will their blessings be.
God has put them to the test
and proved them worthy of glory,
  has tested them like gold in a furnace,
and accepted them as a holocaust.
When the time comes for God's visitation they will shine out;

as sparks run through the stubble, so will they.
They shall judge nations, rule over peoples,
and the Lord will be their king forever.
They who trust in God will understand the truth,
those who are faithful will live forever in love;
for grace and mercy await those God has chosen.
(Wisdom 3:1-9)

Response   Lucien Deiss

Keep in mind that Je-sus Christ has died for us and is ris-en from the

dead. He is our sav-ing Lord, he is joy for all a-ges.

© 1965 World Library Publications. Reprinted with permission.

Alternate the following scripture passages between two readers. Add the sung response from time to time, as indicated.

1: Now we are seeing a dim reflection in a mirror;
   but then we shall be seeing face to face.

2: The knowledge that I have now is imperfect;
   but then I shall know as fully as I am known.   (I Cor. 13:12 JB)

1: The throne of God and of the Lamb will be in its place in the city;
   his servants will worship him, they will see him face to face,
   and his name will be written on their foreheads.

2: It will never be night again and they will not need lamplight or sunlight,
   because the Lord God will be shining on them.
   They will reign for ever and ever.   (Rev. 22:4-5 JB)

Refrain (All)   Keep in mind . . .

1: If in union with Christ we have imitated his death,
   we shall also imitate him in his resurrection.

2: We believe that having died with Christ
   we shall return to life with him.   (Rom. 6:5, 8 JB)

1: What we suffer in this life can never be compared to the glory,
   as yet unrevealed, which is waiting for us.   (Rom. 8:18 JB)

2: Things beyond our seeing, things beyond our hearing,
   things beyond our imagining, all prepared by God for those who love him.
   (I Cor. 2:9 NEB)

Refrain (All)   Keep in mind . . .

1: The Spirit . . . and our spirit bear united witness
   that we are children of God.

104

2: And if we are children we are heirs as well:
heirs of God and coheirs with Christ, sharing his sufferings so as to share his glory.
(Rom. 8:17 JB)

1: My dear people, we are already the children of God
but what we are to be in the future has not yet been revealed;

2: All we know is, that when it is revealed we shall be like him
because we shall see him as he really is.   (I John 3:2 JB)

Refrain (All)   Keep in mind . . .

Reading   The life and death of each of us has its influence on others; if we live, we live for the Lord; and if we die, we die for the Lord, so that alive or dead we belong to the Lord. This explains why Christ both died and came to life, it was so that he might be Lord both of the dead and of the living.   (Rom. 14:7-9 JB)

Response

Reader:	There's a season for everything under the sun,
All:	a time to do and a time to be done,
Reader:	a time to laugh
All:	and a time to cry,
Reader:	a time to live
All:	and a time to die.

(Alternate verses: Readers 1 and 2)

1: A time for dying and a time for rebirth.
2: A time for the spirit and a time for earth.

1: A time for laughter, a time for tears.
2: A time for courage and a time for fear.

1: A time to cling and a time to release.
2: A time for war and a time for peace.

1: A time to talk and a time to be still.
2: A time to care and time to kill.

1: A time alone. A time for romance.
2: A time to mourn. A time to dance.

1: A time to keep. A time to lose.
2: A time to be told. A time to choose.

1: A time to tear down. A time to rebuild.
2: A time to be empty. A time to be filled.

1: A time to welcome and to send away.
2: A time to complain and a time to pray.

1: A time to share and a time to save.
2: A time to break rules. A time to behave.

1: A time to free and a time to bind.
2: A time to search and a time to find.

1: A time to plant and a time to uproot.
2: A time to be barren. A time to bear fruit.

1: A time of plenty.
2: A time of need.

1: A time to follow.
2: A time to lead.

1: A time to give.
2: A time to take.

1: A time to bend.
2: A time to break.

1: A time to hurt.
2: A time to heal.

1: A time for secrets.
2: A time to reveal.

1: A time to let go.
2: A time to hold.

1: A time to be young.
2: A time to grow old.

1: A time to rip open.
2: A time to mend.

1: A time to begin,
2: and a time to end.

(Adapted, from Ecc. 3:1-8*)

Reader:	There's a season for everything under the sun,
All:	a time to do and a time to be done,
Reader:	a time to laugh
All:	and a time to cry,
Reader:	a time to live
All:	and a time to die.

Reading

I tell you most solemnly,
whoever listens to my words,
and believes in the one who sent me,
has eternal life;
without being brought to judgment
.. has passed from death to life.
I tell you most solemnly,
the hour will come—in fact it is here already—
when the dead will hear the voice of the Son of God,
and all who hear it will live.
For the Father, who is the source of life,
has made the Son the source of life;
and, because he is the Son of Man,
has appointed him supreme judge.
Do not be surprised at this,
for the hour is coming
when the dead will leave their graves
at the sound of his voice:
those who did good
will rise again to life;
and those who did evil, to condemnation.
I am the resurrection.
[Whoever] believes in me . . . will live,
and whoever lives and believes in me
will never die.   (John 5:24-29; 11:26 JB)

Response   (All sing the following setting of Psalm 23)

The Lord Is My Shepherd

Response (All sing the following setting of Psalm 23)

Joseph Gelineau

1   My shepherd   the   Lord;   there is
2   He   guides me a - long   the right path;   he   is
3   You have pre - pared   a   banquet   for me   in   the
4   Sure-ly goodness and   kindness shall follow   me   all   the
5   To the Father and   Son   give glory,   give

1 nothing   I shall   want.   Fresh   and   green are the
2 true   to his   name.   If I should walk in   the   valley of
3 sight   of my   foes.   My   head you have a-nointed with
4 days   of my   life.   In the   Lord's own   house shall I
5 glory   to the   Spirit.   To God who   is,   who   was, and who

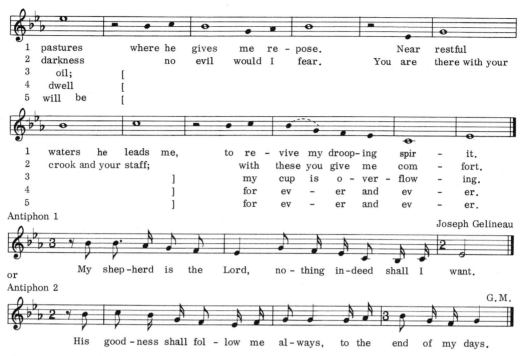

1	pastures		where he	gives	me re - pose.		Near	restful
2	darkness		no	evil	would I	fear.	You are	there with your
3	oil;	[						
4	dwell	[						
5	will be	[						

1	waters	he	leads me,	to re -	vive my droop-ing	spir -	it.
2	crook and your staff;			with	these you give me	com -	fort.
3		]		my	cup is o - ver - flow -		ing.
4		]		for	ev - er and ev -		er.
5		]		for	ev - er and ev -		er.

Antiphon 1

Joseph Gelineau

My shep-herd is the Lord, no - thing in-deed shall I want.

or

Antiphon 2

G.M.

His good-ness shall fol - low me al - ways, to the end of my days.

Copyright © 1959 Ladies of the Grail (England). Used with permission of: G.I.A. Publications, Inc., U.S. Agents, 7404 S. Mason Ave., Chicago, Il. 60638. All rights reserved.

Prayer of the Faithful
+ Spontaneous prayer for the deceased, family, and friends
+ Conclude with the Lord's Prayer recited by all

Benediction

Blessed be the God and Father
  of our Lord Jesus Christ,
  the Father of mercies and the God of all comfort.
Blessed be the Lord who passed from death to life
  that we too might pass over
  to) new mode of being
where life is changed, not taken away,
where death divides no more.
Thanks be to God who gives us the victory
  through our Lord Jesus Christ.
My dear friends, do not be surprised
  at the painful test you are suffering
  as though something unusual
    were happening to you.
Rather be glad that you share Christ's sufferings,
  so that you may be full of joy
  when his glory is revealed.
For as we share abundantly in Christ's sufferings,
  so through Christ we share abundantly in comfort.
May the Lord of peace give you peace at all times
  and in all ways.
      Amen.   (II Cor. 1:3, 5; I Cor. 15:52, 57)
          (I Peter 4:12-13; II Thess. 3:16*)

Song Suggestions

"How I Have Longed" (from the album *Joy Is Like the Rain*), "Night" (see page 53), or "Lovesong" (from the album *Remember Me*)—all by the Medical Mission Sisters. Or "Amazing Grace" or any appropriate song or hymn.

Homecoming

Song   "How I Have Longed" (from the album *Joy Is Like the Rain* by the Medical Mission Sisters)

Call to Prayer This little while
this time between the time Christ came
and comes again
rejoice that ours
is no permanent dwelling here
but an everlasting legacy
with stars.

The content of this prayer reflects a rhythm of scripture, silence, and song, to enable the attentive heart to hear God's Word, savor it, and respond. Holy, Holy, Holy, come, Lord! Each time we sing or say the Sanctus *at a Eucharist, we call on the Lord to come, now, and lead us one step closer to home.*

Scripture

First Reader: Then I saw a new heaven and a new earth; the first heaven and the first earth had disappeared now, and there was no longer any sea. I saw the holy city, the new Jerusalem, coming down from God out of heaven, as beautiful as a bride all dressed for her husband. Then I heard a loud voice call from the throne, "You see this city? Here God lives among people. God will make a home among them; they shall belong to the One who will be their God, whose name is God-with-them. God will wipe away all tears from their eyes; there will be no more death, and no more mourning or sadness. The world of the past is gone." Then the One sitting on the throne spoke: "Now I am making the whole of creation new." (Rev. 21:1-5 based on JB*)

Second Reader: If you love me you will keep my word,
and my Father will love you,
and we shall come to you
and make our home with you.   (John 14:23*)

Silence
Song
Refrain *(All—with or without accompaniment)*

(All - with or without accompaniment)

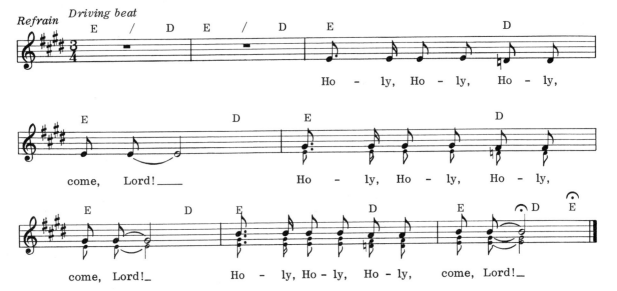

© MCMLXXI by Medical Mission Sisters, Phil., Pa.
Reprinted by permission Vanguard Music Corp., W. 57th St., N.Y., N.Y. 10019

Scripture

> *First Reader:* We know that when this tent we live in—our body here on earth—is torn down, God will have a house in heaven for us to live in, a home [God personally] has made, which will last forever. And now we sigh, so great is our desire that our home which comes from heaven should be put on over us; by being clothed with it we shall not be without a body. While we live in this earthly tent, we groan with a feeling of oppression; it is not that we want to get rid of our earthly body, but that we want to have the heavenly one put on over us, so that what is mortal will be transformed by life. God is the one who has prepared us for this change, . . . gave us the Spirit as the guarantee of all that is in store for us. So we are always full of courage. We know that as long as we are at home in the body we are away from the Lord's home. For our life is a matter of faith, not of sight. We are full of courage and would much prefer to leave our home in the body and be at home with the Lord. More than anything else, however, we want to please [God], whether in our home here or there. (II Cor. 5:1-9 TEV)

> *Second Reader:* Make your home in me,
> as I make mine in you. (John 15:4 JB)

Silence

Song *(All repeat: "Holy, Holy, Holy, come, Lord!")*

Scripture

> *First Reader:* A person will reap exactly what he [or she] plants. If [we sow] in the field of [our] natural desires, from it [we] will gather the harvest of death; if [we] sow in the field of the Spirit, from the Spirit [we] will gather the harvest of eternal life. So let us not become tired of doing good; for if we do not give up, the time will come when we will reap the harvest. So then, as often as we have the chance, we should do good to everyone, and especially to those who belong to our family in the faith. (Gal. 6:7-10 TEV)

> *Second Reader:* If you make my word your home
> you will indeed be my disciples,
> and will learn the truth
> and the truth will make you free. (John 8:32 JB)

Silence

Song *(All repeat: Holy, Holy, Holy, come, Lord!)*
If at all possible, play Hagood Hardy's instrumental piece, "The Homecoming," as the group spends a few final moments in quiet reflection. Use the recorded version, on record or cassette, or have someone in the group play it on the organ or piano. Continue playing softly as background accompaniment to the closing prayer.

Closing Prayer   Blessed be God
the Father of our Lord Jesus Christ,
who in his great mercy has given [us]
a new birth as his sons [and daughters],
by raising Jesus Christ from the dead,
so that [we] have a sure hope
and the promise of an inheritance
that can never be spoiled
or soiled and never fade away,
because it is being kept for you in the heavens.
Through your faith, God's power will guard you
until the salvation which has been prepared

109

is revealed at the end of time.
This is a cause of great joy for you,
even though you may for a short time
have to bear being plagued by all sorts of trials;
so that, when Jesus Christ is revealed,
your faith will have been tested and proved like gold—
only it is more precious than gold,
which is corruptible
even though it bears testing by fire—
and then you will have praise and glory and honor.
You did not see him,
yet you love him;
and still without seeing him,
you are already filled with a joy so glorious
that it cannot be described,
because you believe;
and you are sure of the end to which your faith
looks forward, that is,
the salvation of your souls.
You will have to suffer only for a little while:
the God of all grace
who called you to eternal glory in Christ
will see that all is well again . . .
will confirm, strengthen and support you.
God's power lasts for ever and ever. Amen.

(I Pet. 1:3-9; 5:10-11 JB; format changed by author)

Closing Song Sing a Spiritual that dreams of "crossing over into campground," such as, "Deep River" or "Swing Low, Sweet Chariot." Or any song of longing for the Promised Land, like "Yahweh, the Faithful One" by Dan Schutte, S.J., or "How Lovely" (from the album *Sandstone* by the Medical Mission Sisters).

and so once again
Beginnings

The cycle continues:
   death to life
   day to night and night
      into morning
   birth, rebirth
as feasts, feelings, seasons fuse
to proclaim the Day of the Lord.
Through sorrow to joy
   winter to spring
   Lent into Easter
the child in us
matures in us
   love, life
   begin again
in the daily unfolding promise:
behold, I make all things new.

Prayer is our point of contact
where transcendence penetrates
the core of our commonness
transforming things as they are
to things as they ought to be.
The whole of our experience
permeates our prayer:

   Christ, come quickly!
   Time and again we desperately long
   to cradle the Incarnate
   within our waiting hearts

   know the Cross in our Lenten lows
   of pain and discouragement

   herald Easter emerging
   from every liberation
   significant or small

   celebrate the Spirit
   in those opportunities we take
   to make creation new.

Indeed, at every turn
life links us to the Lord!
At every turn
Love is revealed.
Turn again
and again:
be healed!

ACKNOWLEDGMENTS

The quotations on pages 11 and 12 from *Dawn Without Darkness* by Anthony Padovano. Reprinted by permission of Paulist Press, publishers.

The quotation on page 12 is by Frank Galles and first appeared in *Ebbs and Tidings*, the newsletter of the Sisters of St. Francis, Rochester, Minnesota.

The poetry selections on pages 12, 79, and 111 are from "Gitanjali" from *Collected Poems and Plays* by Rabindranath Tagore. Reprinted with permission of Macmillan Publishing Company, Inc., New York; the Trustees of the Tagore Estate; and Macmillan, London and Basingstoke.

The quotation on page 41 is from *The Eucharist and the Hunger of the World* by Monika Hellwig. Reprinted by permission of Paulist Press, publishers.

The quotation on pages 40-41 is entitled "Hunger" by Miriam Therese Winter, from *Ave Maria*, Oct. 1965, p. 14.

The quotation on page 50 is reprinted from *Letters to a Young Poet* by Rainer Maria Rilke, translated by M. D. Herter Norton. With the permission of W. W. Norton & Company, Inc. Copyright 1935 by W. W. Norton & Company, Inc. Copyright renewed 1962 by M. D. Herter Norton. Rev. Ed. Copyright 1954 by W. W. Norton & Company, Inc. Reprinted also with the permission of St. John's College, London, and Hogarth Press.

The song on page 60, "This Is the Night," by Miriam Therese Winter, is recorded and published in the collection *Remember Me*.

The blessing on page 68 was written by thirty-four-year-old Bill Moody, S. J., for the March, 1974, liturgy at the chapel of the Medical Mission Sisters in Philadelphia. One month later, Bill died.

The quotation on page 70 is excerpted from pages 9, 14-15, of *Eighth Day of Creation* by Elizabeth O'Connor, published in 1971 and used by permission of Word Books, Publisher, Waco, Texas.

The quotation on page 74 is from *The Dome and the Rock*, written by Kenneth Cragg and published by S.P.C.K. in London in 1964.

The quotation on pages 82-83 is from *Free to Be Faithful* by Anthony Padovano. Reprinted by permission of Paulist Press, publishers.

The quotation on page 84 is from *Elements of Hope* by James Carroll. Reprinted by permission of Paulist Press, publishers.

The quotation on page 88 is from *Time and Myth* by John S. Dunne, copyright 1975. Reprinted by permission of Doubleday & Company, publishers.

Music Credits

Words and music in this publication unless otherwise noted are by Miriam Therese Winter and are reprinted by permission of the copyright holders, the Medical Mission Sisters, Philadelphia, Pennsylvania. Songs recorded by the Medical Mission Sisters are available on various albums from Avant Garde Records, Inc., 250 West Fifth-Seventh Street, New York, New York 10019.

The following songs are reprinted by permission of Vanguard Music Corporation, publishers:
—"Spirit of God" on pages 79 and 80, from the collection *Joy Is Like the Rain*

—"Night" on page 53, from the collection *Knock, Knock*

—"Ballad of the Seasons" on page 105, from the collection *Seasons*

—"Yes!" on page 82, from the collection *RSVP*

—"Child of Morning," on page 13, from the collection *Gold, Incense and Myrrh*

—"Living Water" on pages 37-39, "Song of Liberation" on page 66 and "Song of Songs" on pages 95-96, from the collection *Sandstone*

—"Heavenly Father" on page 45, "Rejoice Now! on page 59, "Song of Praise" on page 108, "This Is the Night" on page 60, and "Lovesong" on page 95, from the collection *Remember Me*

The reflection on page 55-56 was written by Loretta Whalen Force for a Good Friday Liturgy with the Medical Mission Sisters.

12   "waiting"

12   [xerox]

83   "transparency"